Qarajeh to Quba

Qarajeh

to Quba

RUGS AND FLATWEAVES FROM EAST AZARBAYJAN AND THE TRANSCAUCASUS

Raoul E. Tschebull

HPL / NEARC

Dedicated to the memory of
Ingeborg Tschebull
W. Russell Pickering
Joseph V. McMullan

Contents

Foreword

Over the past half-century, Transcaucasian carpets of the nineteenth century have been subject to fluctuating fortunes and attention both in the art market and in the world of scholarship. Since the mid-twentieth century, these predominantly small and attractive works of art have been a traditional entryway into carpet collecting, especially in the northeastern United States, where huge numbers of these carpets had found their way in the early twentieth century. They were not only a staple of the rug trade, at that time dominated by Armenian émigrés and Armenian-Americans, but were even sold in the rug departments of major department stores such as Jordan Marsh in Boston. By the 1960s, following the translation into English of Ulrich Schürmann's taxonomic survey of nineteenth century Transcaucasian carpets, the 'Caucasian' rugs showing up in great numbers at antique dealers and country auctions enjoyed great popularity among collectors. Simultaneously, they began to figure prominently in a number of pioneering exhibitions, including the ground-breaking 1961 show *Peasant and Nomad Rugs of Asia* at the Asia Society in New York, curated by Maurice Dimand, and the Finch College show of 1971, also in New York, curated by Raoul Tschebull, that was devoted entirely to Kazak carpets.

In 1975 Charles Grant Ellis published the ground-breaking *Early Caucasian Rugs*, a catalog that accompanied an exhibition of that name at The Textile Museum in Washington, DC. Ellis in effect gave the late nineteenth century rugs from the Caucasus a family history that had already long been present for later rugs of Anatolia and Iran. The emergence in 1978 of HALI magazine, with its substantial attention to carpets woven in the nineteenth century, was another major factor in keeping the later Transcaucasian carpets in the broader picture of carpet study and collecting, especially the latter. Subsequent decades saw the emergence of documentary research in Russian-language sources about pre- and post-Soviet production in Transcaucasia, including new information on flat-woven carpets from this area published by Richard Wright and John Wertime in 1995. Rugs from this area lost some of their cachet as a result, once people realized that the majority of extant examples were fairly recent (late nineteenth century and early twentieth), and that many were the product of organized cottage industries or resulted from Soviet-era economic initiatives designed to bring in much-needed foreign exchange.

Post-Soviet nationalism in the newly independent nations of the Caucasus, as might have been expected, has not brought about a major realignment of scholarly or collecting activity, with the exception of the emergence of newly discovered local products, both pile-woven and flat-woven, from various ethnic groups and geographical areas of the Greater and Lesser Caucasus, that suddenly started to flood western carpet markets after the collapse of the USSR. Long-simmering national and ethnic rivalries, now becoming elements of national policy, in fact have in some cases tended to obscure or impede serious research in the new republics.

Today the time is especially ripe to rise above questions of artistic status and ethnic affiliation and return to a careful look at the works of art themselves. The most promising approach to this material, found in this new book, has been first to winnow and evaluate the available documentary evidence with both caution and detachment; second, to look very carefully at design origins and evolution; and third, to exercise the highest level of aesthetic consensus and evaluation in choosing the works of art to be included and discussed. Carpets from Transcaucasia woven in the nineteenth century comprise a huge number of surviving examples, a vast array of different design and weaving types, and, as with all art, a wide spectrum of artistic quality.

After decades of research focusing not only on the artistic production of traditional Transcaucasian geographical areas, but also on parts of what today's political boundaries classify as north-west Iran, Tschebull adds an important dimension to the broader understanding of his subject by including a significant number of carpets from this region in his study. This should remind us not only of the history of cultural relationships among Azeri-speaking peoples of this area, but also of the significance and the beauty of kindred works of art created 'south of the border'.

At their best, these carpets, from both sides of the border, show us a firm and discernable set of connections to the great traditions of this art form, stretching back many centuries in the available historical record, and undoubtedly further back than that into the unknown and probably unknowable reaches of the past. And at their best, these carpets exemplify the highest level of artistic accomplishment, giving us works of art that in their creative combination of innovation and tradition, in their use of high-quality materials and exquisite colors, and in their eloquence of layout, designs, motifs and colors, can easily be placed in the highest level of artistic accomplishment, reaching out over time and distance to amaze and delight us with their beauty.

Walter B. Denny
Amherst, Massachusetts, 2019

Acknowledgements

In my long trek through the jungle of Islamic rug and textile studies, I have been helped by a myriad of people: Some of the earliest purveyors of wisdom were Russell Pickering, Joseph McMullan and Charles Grant Ellis. Under this august group's wing, I was given a pretty good start. Information came from all directions, including from rug club meetings, curators, visiting individual collectors, the Middle East, long exposure to Moorish Spain, speaking at conferences and benefiting from conference attendee feedback.

Tony Landreau at the Textile Museum was an early source. Siawosch Azadi in Hamburg introduced me to whole new worlds of rug studies. Marilyn Jenkins at the Metropolitan Museum helped me access sophisticated information about Islamic design concepts. Harald Böhmer and Werner Brüggemann provided a model for how to publish a treatise on village rugs from a specific area. In 1985, Dr. Böhmer provided a guided tour of weaving villages in remote parts of western Anatolia for a small group – including me and my wife Ingeborg. The value of anthropological input was made clear. Both Dr. Böhmer and Michael Bischof have made me smarter and more informed with regard to dyeing and the dye process and have emphasized how high-quality dyestuffs and care in the dyeing process produce the most intense color.

Without serious local support in Iran in the late 1990s, I would never have gotten into the 'field' the way I did. Parviz Tanavoli has augmented what I learned in the field, and I am grateful for his knowledge. Marla Mallett has been a long-term guide for structure, and Hamid Sadighi Neiriz in Berlin has helped me to see warp-faced structures with more clarity. John Wertime, among many other things, translated Farsi letters for me. John Howe has provided valuable feedback and has been instrumental in helping to provide a forum at the Textile Museum for my various presentations there. Richard Tapper has been a great source of anthropological information regarding the nomads in East Azarbayjan, referred to as the Shahsavan. Among my contemporaries in the US, two really stand out: Jeff Spurr and Walter Denny.

In the Transcaucasus, insights from Vügar Dadaşov and Shirin Melikova, Director of the Azerbaijan Carpet Museum in Baku, have been valuable. Kubra Aliyeva was a source of crucial information when I visited her in Baku, and Roya Tagiyeva, former Director of the Azerbaijan National Carpet Museum, has provided many digitized photographs of historic Azerbaijan as well as of rugs, *jajims* and textiles in the museum.

I have been helped by knowledgeable people in the rug trade in the US, Turkey, Germany and Iran, and especially by those first-generation New York City carpet dealers, many of them Armenian or Greek. Bob Mann of Robert Mann Rugs in

Colorado has provided insights that only someone with considerable experience in rug weaving areas could have. He has also provided excellent restoration services, and with the wise guidance of New York dealer/restorer Hagop Manoyan, additional outstanding sources were obtained.

Without the support of Danny Shaffer, Ben Evans and HALI magazine/Hali Publications in London over the years, I would never have gotten much into print. Nor could this book have happened without Don Tuttle's painstaking studio photography of my rugs – I appreciate his skills and how easy it was to work with him. Thanks too to Misha Anikst and Ben Strachan of Anikst Design in London for their work, which has helped transform this book into much more than another 'My Rugs by Me' catalogue of a private collection.

This book is published under the auspices of the Near Eastern Art Research Center (NEARC), a private foundation established in 1962 by Joseph V. McMullan to provide support in the early phases of publications in the field of Islamic carpets.

Raoul E. Tschebull
Darien, Connecticut, 2019

Introduction

Through chance and opportunity, I have collected mostly nineteenth-century pile rugs and pile-less weavings from adjoining regions – an area in northwestern Iran that has been known as East Azarbayjan, plus the Transcaucasus and part of Dagestan. My interest is in the rural and village textile material culture that is centered on largely unsupervised weaving – almost the opposite of most 'classical' and 'city' rugs and carpets.

Although the geographic areas are contiguous and were one more or less unified administrative entity until the beginning of the nineteenth century, they are quite different, one from the other. A substantial difference is that the weaving culture in East Azarbayjan was not disrupted by invasions and occupation in the nineteenth century and could be studied without allowing for the effects resulting from outside conquest. And since the area had active nomad, village, and city workshop weaving communities until comparatively recent times, there is a great variety of woven material as well as anthropological, cultural and commercial information to consider.

I have always been fascinated by the prospect of understanding the various inputs into this weaving culture, even if on a less than perfect basis. For years I wrote about the weavings from afar, but eventually wangled two periods of field work in rural East Azarbayjan in the late summers of 1996 and 1997.

The kind of access I wanted was not easy to obtain. However, it was possible, with the essential help of Iranian contacts, for me to explore remote historic weaving villages and several nomad encampments pretty thoroughly, to meet with locals and get a good feel for why they live the way they do. It was not the long-term study typically carried out by professional anthropologists, but it was more specialized. Almost any amount of informed personal experience in situ can be illuminating, and the combination of field exposure and analysis at home of these antique textiles provides a more balanced picture. To help describe this area, its inhabitants and living conditions, to set the scene as I saw it in the mid to late 1990s, I have included abridged and edited comments from my field notes at appropriate places in the texts below.

The Transcaucasus was invaded and taken over by the Russians beginning in about 1800, and the output of pile-woven rugs, especially, grew in volume over the next hundred years. However, there is comparatively little known about pre-'rug boom' production, one of my major interests. Such rugs can be the equal of any other group of Turkish or Iranian village weaving.

The real Transcaucasian boom seems to have been mostly a late nineteenth century phenomenon. Supporting this idea is the rather naive first book published discussing the purchase of Transcaucasian village rugs, in 1884, by Herbert Coxon, *Oriental Carpets; How They Are Made and Conveyed to Europe*, and additionally, the fact that a preponderance of rugs with in-woven dates are from close to 1900.

It is probable that the increase in the export of Transcaucasian rugs was stimulated by the completion in 1884, as described by Coxon, of a railway from Baku to Batumi on the Black Sea, bypassing the arduous overland route used previously. By studying Transcaucasian rugs with late in-woven dates and comparing them with undated examples, it is possible to some extent to correlate color and design from dated pieces to figure out how old undated pieces are.

From a folklife aspect, these Transcaucasian weavings have been viewed locally mostly through a relatively late Tsarist/Soviet lens. A rewarding way to study them focuses on taxonomy, which is not open to distortion.[1] And understanding structure is critical. For me, technical analysis of every piece illustrated in this collection helps give mute objects a voice.

In parallel with taxonomy, I am interested how pile weaving designs evolved and what the sources were in both East Azarbayjani and Transcaucasian weaving, as well as how dye sources and use changed and how export markets affected formats and structure. With regard to pile-less flatwoven *kilims* and *jajims*, the interest is that they remained relatively stable in the face of demand pressure on pile rugs, how their motifs, plus those in local silk embroideries, influenced pile weaving, how flatweave structure often drove pile rug design, how universal some pile-less weaving designs are in these pile rugs, and how and why dye use in these textiles differed from those used in pile rugs.

There is not much 'unique' in these mostly rural and small-town weaving cultures, which is to be expected, but many of the 'folk art' pieces in this study seem to be so. That is probably a function of more complex older pieces having been produced in fewer numbers, under less commercial pressure, and many more of them having been worn out than later pieces. Differentiation of quality is largely a result of weavers' color sensibility, combined with their ability to push the design envelope within a set of conservative cultural values.

Collectors of Eurasian rugs and textiles have varying color perceptions and different specific areas of geographic and design interest. A major focus here is on color variety and my perception of intensity. Different people have different ideas of what good color and design are, and it has nothing to do with character judgement. However, there are good, better, best rug and textile perceptions that seem to be held by a majority, establishing a semi-unified idea of value.

Most weaving of this type is done by younger women whose eyesight is good and whose backs are strong. So, if the craft is not passed on to younger people, it can degenerate fairly quickly. This factor, probably on the margin, contributed to the rapid decline of Transcaucasian rug weaving quality toward the end of the nineteenth century.

The question arises that if the rug looks right and is an honest weaving, why is age important? It should be noted that I do not jump on age like many people in this field do. Why do good reproductions sell for much less than genuinely old rugs? A rug can be late and very good. Unfortunately, however, the problem of fakes made to deceive occurs with increasing regularity. Suffice to say that the vast majority of these illustrated pieces were bought over many years, beginning in the 1960s, before values shot up and fakes became a hot topic – or were bought by me as an experienced 'insider' with long-standing relationships in the rug collecting and dealing communities.

I am interested in pile-woven rugs because of the texture, tapestry weaves because of the broad areas of color they afford, and *jajims* because of their function, color and how their restrictive weaves have had an influence on pile-woven rugs.

The motivation to write this treatise is at least threefold: learn more about my material through research and networking; leave a record of what I have collected and why; and pass on what I have learned as a collector. Or as my friend Russ Pickering succinctly described the collecting process, '1. Search and Seizure; 2. Study and Analysis; and 3. Stewardship (the writing part)'.

This study can serve as a guide to a narrow but very interesting sector of Eurasian weavings. It is set up as an illustrated narrative – almost a 'stream-of- consciousness' approach – about knotted-pile rugs, tapestry-woven *kilims* and warp-faced *jajims* – but only tangentially about the region's mainly *sumak* transport bags – and is meant to be both a presentation of a private collection and a specialist's particular view of this art form. A *leitmotif* running through the plate descriptions are constant rhetorical questions – implied and direct – and comments on the lack of cultural information, especially with regard to weavings from the Transcaucasus.

In my text, I cite as many insights and opinions as I can attribute – I do not want to steal others' specific ideas – but knowledge in this field is diffuse, often orally transmitted, seldom carefully documented, and often cannot be attributed to individuals.

Plate descriptions do not describe what the reader can see, rather, they explain mainly taxonomy, color and design origination and evolution, as well as social and commercial considerations. There is a lot of 'compare and contrast' in the plate descriptions, but this is a pretty standard art historical approach, and is useful for deeper understanding.

The rugs and textiles illustrated here are examples of types, and the descriptions and insights are meant to have some application to a broader area of rug and textile study, to augment what has already been published.

Etymology, Transliteration & Definitions

A very good place to start is a definition for the Transcaucasus, which is the area between the Caucasian mountain chain and the Iranian border. It is originally a Russian construct.[2] In the context of this study, it includes a part of southern Dagestan. Azerbaijan, the name of the present-day republic in the Transcaucasus, where most 'Caucasian' rugs were woven, is a separate entity from (West or) East Azarbayjan, the adjoining provinces in northwest Iran. This spelling – Azarbayjan – has been current in Roman characters in Iran for decades. In this text, for simplicity's sake, I often use 'Caucasian' instead of 'Transcaucasian' and 'Azarbayjani' instead of 'East Azarbayjani', but the definition remains the same.

Many names that have been spelled in English beginning with a 'K' are now starting with a 'Q', and sometimes, a 'G'. That is because Iranian village names are sometimes pronounced very little like the existing English or German transliteration. To add to the confusion, G's, Q's and K's are not used on a consistent basis. And there is always room for freelance spelling. A good example is 'Karaja' or 'Karadja'. A better approximation of how the name sounds locally works out to be 'Qarajeh' or 'Garajeh', with the emphasis on the last syllable. After patiently listening to the Azarbayjanis pronounce it, I think the best transliteration seems to be 'Qarajeh'.

There are various ways to spell the terms for large, long, pile-woven rugs in Iran: those approximately 3'6" × 10'–15' (110 × 300–450 cm) are '*kennereh*'; larger, wider pieces, say, 5' × 10'–12' (150 × 300–350 cm) or so are '*kelleh*'. They are not 'runners' but were woven in these formats to fit specific spaces in their local environments. It is probably better to think of rugs in these formats as 'long rugs.' Much folk art weaving is in long format.

'Folk art' is used here to differentiate between weavings reflecting primarily local rural traditions and those with export-driven patterns. The separation is of course, a bit fuzzy.

There are myriad invented and local terms for motifs, some of which are probably accurate. I have generally avoided using them because they do not add much to the narrative.

The word '*mafrash*' is apparently an Arab loan word, meaning furniture, and is in common use in Iran to describe box-like bedding bags used for transport by nomads. A Turki word for the same object is '*farmesh*' and seems more applicable for nomads in the area under discussion here.

The term 'flatwoven' (or 'flatweave), applied to a whole class of pile-less Transcaucasian and Azarbayjani textiles, is not generally used by museum professionals, but is an apt description, commonly used in the rug and related textile community. I try, for simplicity's sake, to limit the use of most arcane in-country terms, often conflicting with one another, for various flatwoven structures.

Lastly, a common weft wrapping technique has been labelled '*sumakh*', as if it were a name derived from local cultures, with an aspirated 'h'. It appears in several different spellings and seems to be an entirely made up appellation. Some think the technique's name is derived from the town of Shamakhi in the Transcaucasus, but it is used widely to describe products from distant weaving areas in Eurasia.[3] An alternative is '*qayeq*', cited as a local term by Jenny Housego,[4] and I remember Roya Tagiyeva, former Director of the Azerbaijan National Carpet Museum in Baku, using a version of it to describe weft wrapping. The term may be derived from the large local tribal group, the Geyiklu. Instead I use '*sumak*'.

Materials & Techniques

These textiles were primarily woven – not embroidered – with animal fiber – sheep's wool, goat hair, and silk. Warps and wefts in these weavings are majority wool, but cotton was used as available. Their spin and ply are described as mostly two and three Z-spun strands plied S. The term 'singles', used to define weft material, describes a 'Z' strand, and 'shots', a weaver's term, passes of weft between rows of knots. Some cotton warps are four Z strands plied S. All pile knotting in this collection is symmetrical (so called 'Turkish') and is well sorted and combed Z2S wool from several different breeds of sheep. Density is shown in inches and centimeters, using an average from several locations. It is said that good rug weavers try to have warp and weft knot count be roughly the same but, clearly, there are good looking pile rugs with divergent knot symmetry.

Regarding the origin of pile-woven rugs, it is easy to accept the idea that pile weaving represents a substitute for animal skins with fur or wool surfaces – especially for nomads in Central Asia, who had less access to fur. It probably evolved subsequent to felt making.[5] Given their lifestyle, during the nineteenth century settled people in higher elevation areas in the Azarbayjan/Transcaucasus region would, for the most part, have used felts, felt-backed flatweaves or thick pile rugs to sit on, not pile-less *sumak* or other brocaded structures. The latter simply do not wear very well. An exception to this preference was the culture that valued large *sumak* rugs and carpets in the northeast part of Azerbaijan and Dagestan.

For warp-faced tapestry woven pieces ('*kilim*' in the Transcaucasus, '*gilim*' in Iran), as well as for those that are warp-faced (*jajims*), warp and weft density are also in inches and centimeters. With pile-woven rugs, warps lie more or less on one level, unless otherwise noted. Pile length at its highest is shown in millimeters because it is a more sensitive measure than inches for things like pile. Pile colors are listed in approximate order of usage; ivory pile is natural undyed wool unless otherwise noted. '*Abrash*' (color variation within a block of color) is only counted as one separate color. Selvedges and end finishes, when still in place, are described using Marla Mallett's weaver's terminology.[6]

It should be noted that some 'high quality' rugs in this collection have either elaborately colored selvedges, using most or all the colors found in the pile portion of the rug (Plates 3, 16, 28, 38, 40, 42), or an unusual expensive color for selvedges and plainweave end finishes (Plate 56). It is hard to escape the impression that such treatment denotes special care on the part of the weaver, relating to time and place and/or artistic talent.

Color

Dyes have not been chemically analyzed. It is a destructive process and there is generally no intent here to prove age on the basis of dyes or C-14 (radiocarbon dating) studies. The objects in this study reflect rural color sensitivity, wherein local dyers used a variety of 'natural' dyes and mordants. Dye and fiber analysis techniques are advancing all the time, and will probably, in time, allow non-invasive tests to provide accurate production dates for rugs and textiles. But the first question asked when viewing these objects should not be 'How old?' but, rather, how attractive and interesting.

Nomads in the Transcaucasus and East Azarbayjan likely had the wool they used for weaving dyed when during migrations they passed through villages and towns with dye shops. As evidence of this, the similarities in color between village pile rugs and nomad *sumak*, warp-faced, various types of brocades and slit-tapestry weaves are usually very close. For nomads to haul around dyeing material and pots would have been quite a logistic chore. Alternatively, dyers could have visited nomads in summer camps and done their work there. Other specialists, like felt makers, travelled from camp to camp in the summer, so it is not impossible that some professional dyeing could have been done the same way.

With regard to dye quality, what jumps out is how the variety and intensity of dyes declined over the nineteenth century, especially in the Transcaucasus. I will never be a dye chemist but have spent years learning about the process of using 'natural' dyes in Eurasian weaving. There are said to be myriad additives and processes that enhanced dye color in early periods when there was less haste.

RUSSIA
Greater Caucasus
Black Sea
GEORGIA
Lesser Caucasus
Kura
Batumi
Tibilisi
BORCHALI
Kura
Kazak
Akstafa
Pambak
Kars
ARMENIA
Lake Sevan
Yerevan
Aras Nehri
Aras
TURKEY
Divrigi
Qarabagh
Van Golu
Daryacheh-Ye Orumiyeh
IRAQ
0 20 40 60 80 100 Miles
0 20 40 60 80 100 120 140 160 180 km

Caspian Sea
DAGESTAN
Derbent
Zaqatal
Zeikhur
Alpan
Quba
Sheki
Kura
Shamakhi
Maraza
Bijov
Baku
Talish
AZERBAIJAN
Kura
Araks
Shirvan
Shusha
Sal'yan
Bahmanli
MOGHAN
Kura
Jabrayil
Araks
Qara Su
Ahar
Mount Sabalan
Meshkin Shahr
Qarajeh
Heriz
Ardabil
Tabriz
Bakshaish
Mehraban
Duzduzan
Mount Sahand
Bostanabad
Sarab
Bozgush Mountains
Qarehchaman
Miyaneh
EAST AZARBAYJAN
Zanjan
IRAN
Tehran

East Aza

rbayjan

Historic East Azarbayjan – *Azarbayjan-e-Sharq* – is more or less the size of the US state of West Virginia (62,000 square km) and borders the Transcaucasus in the north. In 1993, the eastern province of Ardabil was hived off, but for the purposes of this narrative the term 'East Azarbayjan' applies to the original entity. It is an interesting area of study, since it has been the home of early court weaving, substantial urban production of export rugs and carpets, village weaving for local use and export, and then there were nomads, who, up until comparatively recent times, wove objects for their own use and occasionally, sale.

> *Physical description, field notes:* When first setting out on an extensive fact-finding trip through rural East Azarbayjan, we roll into the center of Sarab, a dusty, ugly, large town with a metropolitan population of about 140,000, and stop in a restaurant. In the entranceway on the wall is the best map of East Azarbayjan I have ever seen, with topographic detail to die for. I want a copy, since all I have is my own large map of Iran, which has lots of place names but no elevation details. A member of our party of four asks about availability for me, and the owner, ever obliging, like virtually all Iranians I meet, rummages around in a closet and finds a battered, dog-eared copy of the same large map, and presents it to me with a smile. I'm overjoyed, and pore over it while eating my *chelo kabab*. The larger place names are all in Roman characters, and distances are metric.[7]
>
> Most of this roughly square-shaped province is relatively high in altitude except for parts of the Moghan, which is almost at sea level. Tabriz is at almost 1400 meters, Sarab at 1650, and Heriz, Mehreban, Bakshaish, and Qarajeh also at 1600–1700 meters. Ahar is in a valley in Qaradagh, in the mountains, but is situated only at an elevation of 1160 meters. The distance from Tabriz to both Sarab and Ahar is about 130 km and, on average, the province is about 350 km across.
>
> East Azarbayjan is dominated by two mountain massifs, which are volcanic in origin, but now dormant. Directly south of Tabriz is Sahand, which is roughly a circle on a map, but appears as a jagged massif from the Tabriz-Bostanabad road. The Sabalan massif, further east, and at about 4600 meters, one of the highest mountains in Iran, is about 50 km long, stretching roughly between Ahar on the west and Ardabil on the east, and appears to have had its top blown off at some point in the distant past. From Tabriz east, there is a wide central valley along which runs the main road. About 50 km east of Tabriz, at Bostanabad, where the narrow east–west

Late summer, 1996, approaching a village in upland East Azarbayjan, with the tops of 'Tabrizis' (Lombardy poplars) visible in the distance.

3100-meter Bozgush Mountains begin[8], the valley forks, with a subsidiary valley on the north side of the Bozgush running east to Ardabil, and the one on the south side pointed southeast toward Miyaneh, Zanjan, and ultimately, Tehran. The dreaded Tabriz-Tehran road runs through Miyaneh, and the drive, which is 650 km, takes 8½ hours if everything goes right.

My travels were largely in the wide valley complex between the Bozgush on the south, the Sabalan massif and the high mountains of Qaradagh on the north. It is, in a few places, like around Sarab, perfectly flat and 10 km wide, but in other areas, it rises slightly and is not cultivated. The low places are intensively farmed; grain crops were already harvested by late August, but there were cabbages, potatoes, melons, and tomatoes in the fields, and cattle everywhere. Flocks of sheep and goats graze the odd unplanted area, as well as the grain field stubble. Donkeys are common, and are used for transport, riding and draught purposes. I saw four donkeys yoked together, walking in a circle, dragging a harrow-like implement, cutting up dried hay for fodder.

Mud brick structures in the small village of Gorevan, late summer, 1997. Note the protruding 'Tabrizi' roof joists, flat roofs, and far from any wetland, geese which provide meat and eggs.

But I saw few horses. There are buffalo, which are used for heavy field work. Massey-Ferguson, and above all, John Deere tractors and harvesters are on the roads and in the fields.

There is very little surface water, partly because August is the height of the dry season. A few streams trickle in the valley, but there is no large river, and even very few dry river beds, even though the map shows a small river meandering west toward Tabriz. Crops are irrigated by water pumped from the subsoil aquifer into primitive channels, which are used to flood fields, and are controlled by hand-operated gates. I wonder how much pumping this valley can stand and have heard that the water table in many parts of Iran is severely drawn down. My host in East Azarbayjan later said that efficient use of water is an important national goal to be reached over the next ten years.

The completely level areas were probably wetlands or lakes that might have been drained as early as Neolithic times, and the fertility of such an area must have supported a community where present day Sarab is, for some time. The volcanic ash-based soil is itself very fertile, but it blows everywhere in the constant wind, and one's shoes are soon gray from the ash. The hillsides are beautifully layered in yellow sandstone, limestone, gray-white ash, black ash, and red hematite. South-facing slopes are noticeably more weathered, due to sun exposure and constant freeze-thaw cycles, and north-facing villages have an easier time of it.

There are no naturally-growing trees or shrubs on south-facing slopes, and scrub oak forests grow on some slopes facing north. The uncultivated areas support only grass and woody herbs, like vetch and thyme. In every damp spot that is not occupied by a village, there are planted Lombardy poplars, called 'Tabrizis' by the locals. These grow to, at most, two feet in diameter and up to about forty feet high and provide the construction material used for housing – as well as for looms and charcoal. The narrow, weak upper trunks of 'Tabrizis' are used extensively as heddle rods by weavers.

It is amazing that there are no trees at all on many hillsides, but millennia of grazing by sheep and goats must have eliminated them. Some southern exposures may never have been forested. I suppose there would have been conifer cover at higher altitudes at one point, but almost certainly, it, too, was eliminated by grazing, beginning many years ago. The tree line in Azarbayjan is close to 2500 meters, so elevation seems to play no part in the lack of high-altitude tree cover.

One consequence of the lack of any natural vegetation other than grass is a remarkable lack of bird life. Only flocks of Eurasian crows are common, and even magpies are scarce.

The east-west valley between the Bozgush mountain range and Sabalan rises about 35 km east of Sarab, and there is a series of ridges and canyons through which the eastbound road forms tortuous switchbacks before coming down to a much lower elevation at a town called Nir. There, one sees the headwaters of the Qarasu, which is the size of, and looks like, a medium-sized European trout stream. There are Iranian families picnicking on the banks and washing their cars. This river, the major one in East Azarbayjan, runs 180 degrees in a semi-circle around the Sabalan massif, flowing east, then north, then west, before heading down into the Moghan to empty into the Aras. The only other actively flowing river I saw is the Ahar Chai, the major tributary to the Qarasu, which rises in Qaradagh and flows eastward through the city of Ahar. The Qarasu valley forms a logical path for caravans to have used to transport goods from the Caucasian settlements to Tabriz. There are old caravansarai along this route.

> We saw rainstorms in the distance during the day and got sprinkled on once or twice while in the valley. The major precipitation seems to come in the fall and winter. It is said by many that snowfall in Sarab is very heavy, and that the temperature reaches minus 30 degrees Centigrade. Sarab often has the coldest temperatures in Iran. The implication is that nomads did not winter in this area between Tabriz and Sarab, because it was too cold and there was no grass for their flocks. The Moghan Shahsavan are said to have come down to Sarab in former times, probably to spring and fall markets. As I absorbed my lessons in geography, it became clear that the Shahsavan and many other Azarbayjani nomads wintered in the Moghan or in the middle reaches of the Qarasu.

At one time, there were an estimated 70,000–90,000 nomads living in the area, but the settled portion of the population in the nineteenth century outnumbered the nomads by a factor said to be 7:1, which helped steer the concentration in this collection toward village pile weaving. The larger town and village names in East Azarbayjan are fairly well known, but the inhabitants of many smaller villages that at one time surely wove distinctive rugs, no longer weave much of anything. And there is little institutional memory. Sometimes, reasonably old rugs can be found in mosques that identify local village patterns, but not very often. There are occasional old *jajims* and *gilims*, but there is not much elderly pile weaving, even in fragmented form, in village houses.

The normal formats for village pile weaving were long and narrow, both because they fit into their long narrow living spaces and because they could be woven by one or two weavers. In a village house, pile rugs were sat upon in communal spaces, and were originally quite long pile, to protect from the cold. Most were wool, but there is an account of goat hair very long pile rugs in use also.

> *Housing in Azarbayjani villages, field notes:* Some houses in larger villages like Mehreban have brick exterior load-bearing walls, which make it possible for roof joists to be laid almost directly on the walls. However, more common in rural Azarbayjan is the use of mud brick for exterior walls, which cannot bear weight, and forces the use of post and beam construction. Poplar posts, beams and joists are used in their natural, unsawn state, sometimes even without the bark peeled off. Posts around the perimeter of a house support beams as a framework, and roof joists lie across the beams. Most poplar logs used for framing are not very long, maybe 12 feet at the most, with the length

limited by the soft, weak quality of the wood, and this usually limits a single room to about ten feet of interior width. If a double width room is desired, that is, 20 feet wide – and they exist in a few homes – an elaborate system of interior posts and beams must be constructed down the center of that room. As a consequence, most common, or living rooms we visited were ten feet wide and up to 20 feet long. There is no structural limitation to room length.

Mud is mixed with chopped straw to form square, thin bricks, about 8" × 10" (20 × 25 cm), which sun-dry and are then used for exterior walls. I saw no brick molds, so the bricks must be hand-formed. One sees piles of these bricks in a village, as construction is going on actively at this point in the dry season. After walls are built, mud slurry, with chopped straw added, is plastered onto walls over bricks. I saw this being done in Qarajeh. The process must be repeated at least once a year. Roofs must be reworked with stucco more often. The flat roof, built up of layers of poplar beams, mud and smaller pieces of wood, is the vulnerable point in these village houses: Eventually, the build-up of stucco on the roof is so great, the house can collapse from the weight, or else it all has to be taken down and replaced. Heavy rain can be a disaster. We saw collapsed and abandoned mud brick houses, but many such still-inhabited structures were said to be hundreds of years old, especially village mosques.

Next to the piles of mud bricks in an Azarbayjani village, there are often piles of cow manure bricks, also drying in the sun. In the wet season they are covered with mud and straw. I saw cow dung bricks being made up by women wearing gauntleted heavy blue rubber gloves. Although there is some compressed gas used for cooking, and some kerosene heaters are used, the main cold season heat source is cow dung bricks, used in *tanurs*. It is said by travelers in the Middle East that these bricks burn clean and very hot.

The area is known for the use of undyed beige sheep's wool for domestic weaving purposes – call it the 'Sarab' style. Beige rugs can be seen in most houses – often woven with subdued use of bright red; this seems to have been based on local color perception, not loss of dye technology.

There are islands of rugs in East Azarbayjan with saturated color and no beige wool, like those in the 'Qarajeh' style. It is hard to localize many of these brighter colored rugs. Some are probably a result of in-migration from Kurdistan to the south, Transcaucasian peoples from the north, and settled nomads using their own color sensitivities to weave pile rugs.

A curious comparison between the pile weavings of East Azarbayjan and the Transcaucasus is that while I understand the rural culture and can deduce how it functioned in the nineteenth century in East Azarbayjan, I cannot localize many of the brighter colored rugs; with regard to Transcaucasian weaving, it is the opposite. To muddy the waters further, there are a few pile rugs from Qarabagh in the Transcaucasus, woven in the 'Sarab' beige wool style, with typical pendant medallions. It seems probable that such anomalies owe their existence to population movements of settled peoples north across the river dividing the Transcaucasus from East Azarbayjan.

Add to the domestic, originally not-for-export, weaving style, a whole class of pile rugs and carpets produced for sale, mostly in the West. These can be beautiful, with designs based on local imagery combined with formats demanded by importers and often with brighter colors than 'Sarabs' have. Local village dye shops were quite good at producing clear natural dyes with a high level of saturation for these rugs up into the 1920s, much later than their Transcaucasian counterparts. There are four export-like Azarbayjani rugs illustrated in this collection (Plates 15–18).

There is a wholesale tendency to ascribe intensely colored as well as camel-colored geometric design pile weaves from the area to the 'Shahsavan' (nomad) tribal confederation in East Azarbayjan. However, nomads (now seasonal, moving about on 4-wheel drive trucks or tractors pulling wagons) that I talked with identified themselves by individual tribal names, and said further that there was no tradition of weaving pile objects. It was said that the nomads acquired pile rugs from settled people. Richard Tapper, the preeminent Shahsavan scholar, has the same opinion,[9] as does Jenny Housego, who writes 'The Shahsevan seem to have been little concerned with pile rugs, and there are few pieces that can be authoritatively attributed to them.'[10]

It is most likely that the great majority of 'Shahsavan' pile weaving is village sourced. There are a number of reasons for this opinion, aside from the numbers game embedded in the population imbalance; these nomads typically moved every 10 to 14 days to meet grazing needs, so textiles had to be woven quickly, which precludes most pile, which is more labor and capital intensive, takes longer to weave. Transport bags had to be lightweight and therefore easily transportable and were therefore pile-less tapestry, warp-faced, brocaded or *sumak* in construction. Nomads simply did not have the skill set, nor the market knowledge, to weave pile-woven articles.

Young Moghanlu nomad woman weaving a small *sumak* rug in a felt-covered *kume* at about 2200 meters elevation, late summer, 1996. Dyed wool and probably also pattern are all supplied by an Iranian government agency that encourages handicrafts. Note the traditional knock-down wooden loom.

Settled nomads mostly would not have been called Shahsavan but were likely substantial weavers of *sumak* as well as pile-woven bags for the market (it may be useful for collectors interested in this field to divide the products of this weaving culture between 'settled peoples' and 'nomads'). Based on museum acquisition data, they were being bought in the local markets for sale to collectors around 1900.[11] Regarding specific settled nomad pile weaving, in-country lore has it that pile rugs in smaller long rug format were woven by settled Geyiklu nomads north of Ardabil; they have intense colors and a very 'nomady' feel.

None of this detracts from the beauty of *sumak* bags from East Azarbayjan and/or the Transcaucasus, nor from rugs and carpets woven for export.

Some of the most compelling textiles in this collection are warp-faced covers called *jajims*, woven by both nomads and villagers, and used as felt-backed ground cloths, bedding covers, pack covers during migration, and animal covers.

1

Size	3'6" × 13'3" (107 × 404 cm)
Warp	Z4S undyed cotton, alternate warps slightly depressed
Weft	Two singles, undyed cotton, two shots, plus random dark brown wool singles
Knotting	V 8, H 8, 64/square inch, 992/square dm; pile height about 4mm
Selvedges	Two pairs of reinforced warps interlaced with aubergine and beige wool
Ends	Warp finishes missing, outside barber's pole border missing
Colors	9: medium beige, abrashed rose, light beige, dark aubergine, medium blue, light rose, blue green, ivory, brown/black

Related example: McMullan, 1965, plate 27
Published: Tschebull, 1995, plate 14

'Bakshaish' long rug, *kennereh*

The field decoration is a deconstructed version of an earlier Kurdish workshop design. It echoes the palmettes, rosettes and ogival elements which sprout apparent lily forms in those large carpets, which are well illustrated in rug literature. The diagonal arrow-like forms here seem to have jumped out of the workshop version's palmettes and onto adjoining plant forms that have nothing to do with that particular large carpet style. The arrow-like forms apparently originated within palmettes on Ottoman voided silk velvets as small flowers on long stems.

The ancestral Kurdish large carpet design, itself inspired by earlier workshop examples, has several derivative versions that were more popular in the Transcaucasus than in East Azarbayjan, sometimes also with a 'Kufic' border. The 'Kufic' border in this weaving is precisely drawn, in contrast to the relaxed field decoration, but has a different color combination from the Caucasian norm. The Kufesque motif is drawn from other media, even stucco, and is not really readable as Kufic script.[12]

Kennereh – long, relatively narrow format, pile woven rugs, circa 3'6" × 10' plus – could have been woven in any number of villages in East Azarbayjan, but the less dense construction and the use of rose tones may point to Bakshaish, which is one of the larger towns in the area, as the source. It was woven sometime in the nineteenth century.

The combination of soft tonality dyes in this rug is typical for much of the rural domestic pile weaving culture in East Azarbayjan and is fairly consistent throughout the nineteenth century, even right up to a bit past 1900. The beige field color here is slightly corroded and therefore may be dyed or, more likely, heavily washed, as opposed to the more common undyed uncorroded brown/beige wool used in these rugs.

The beige wool used comes for the most part from village sheep herds, which, on the basis of personal observation, are more mixed in color than those of nomads. Nomads (now transhumant) in high altitude Qaradagh in northwest Iran, were and are stock breeders, and usually have herds of almost all white sheep, again, based on personal observation. White wool has more market value than beige.

The cotton foundation can be an age indicator, but in this case, probably not, based on the rug's structure, coloration and drawing. Cotton was used for warps and sometimes wefts, starting from well before this rug was woven. Z4S warps, as in this piece, indicate that this rug may indeed have been woven in a larger town, like Bakshaish, with sources for multi-ply warps typically used in large carpet production.

2

Size	3'9" × 14'10" (114 × 452 cm)
Warp	Z2S beige wool
Weft	Two singles, rose/pink wool, two shots
Knotting	8.5 V, 7 H, 59.5 knots/square inch, 922/square dm; pile height about 4mm
Selvedges	Two pairs of warps interlaced with red wool
Ends	Warp finishes missing
Colors	12: maroon, ivory, red, medium green, rose, light green, blue green, medium blue, yellow, very dark blue, brown/black, aubergine

Published: Tschebull, 1995, plate 13

'Sarab' long rug, *kennereh*

Although not structurally related to the previous piece, this rug shares the use of Kufesque elements, but in this case escaped from the border tradition, and the same diagonal arrow-like devices.

The coloration – a combination of dark (maroon-like) and light rosy red madder dyes, and the lack of beige – sets it apart from other pendant medallion *kennereh* from the Sarab area. In my experience, only one old really red 'Sarab' has made an appearance, years ago in a California dealer's inventory. There are few old rugs like this one, some in fragmented form, and they usually have a dark beige field coloration, but use the same rosy red dyes as secondary colors.

It is not possible to know which village this cluster of pile rugs comes from, but it was probably (generously) somewhere in the triangle between Qarehchaman, west of Sarab, Ahar to the north, and as far southeast as Miyaneh. My field notes describe villagers saying that in many small towns, weavers ceased producing pile *kennereh* many years ago, so pieces like this one could have been woven in a village that has not been weaving for generations and has no institutional memory of prior weaving traditions.

The design is a combination of an urban motif – the '*Herati*' pattern of rosettes and leaves sourced originally from Safavid workshops – and a version of the standard Sarab pendant medallion. The '*Herati*' on maroon does not quite work right and the complex design seems not to have been taken from a cartoon.

This style of 'Sarab' seems hardly to have been produced as an export rug. Only one late piece has turned up, which has a cotton foundation, aubergine dyes and a much-simplified design.

3

Size	3'0" × 9'10" (91 × 300 cm)
Warp	Z2S ivory/beige wool
Weft	Two singles, ivory/beige wool, four shots
Knotting	5 V, 8 H, 40 knots/square inch, 620/square dm; pile height about 8mm
Selvedges	Two pairs of reinforced warps interlaced in segments with aubergine, red, blue and yellow wool
Ends	Warp finishes missing
Colors	7: ivory, medium blue, pale to bright red, aubergine, yellow, teal, dark brown

Related example: Grogan, Boston, Rudnick sale, November 2016, Lot 20

Azarbayjani (?) long rug, *kennereh*

There are long format plain field *kilims* with large reciprocal outside borders very much like this pile woven rug, that may have served as *sofreh* – a spread on which food would be served. Probable design predecessors were Central Asian appliqué and mosaic felts with similar wide borders. Mosaic felts – 'non-woven textiles' – by their very nature, may have been the basis for the 'negative space' – the ambiguity of background and foreground – that this main border implies to the viewer.

This rug seems to follow that same felt and tapestry weave border tradition, if in a different medium, but with field decoration. It is long pile, multi-wefted, and light-weight and would have made reasonable floor covering to sit on in an Azarbayjani common room, but not very durable if woven as an export rug. There are very few rugs like this one and to know exactly where it was woven is not possible, other than to surmise East Azarbayjan. 'Runners' were in any case not very lucrative to produce commercially. Consequently, for long rugs, there was less commercial pressure, and, in any case, rural weaving folkways were better preserved than in the Caucasus. The lack of comparables may reflect age, as does an old aubergine in purple gray tones. Ascending plant forms on ivory probably relate to imported Kashmiri or Indian textiles, and likely date this piece to post 1800.

Most of the guard borders and ends were rewoven about forty years ago, before I owned the rug, and long before good rug restoration was widely available and reasonable: the quality of the work is astounding. The question of whether to restore – or not – yields no easy answers and has been an issue in art circles since at least the Renaissance.

'Qarajeh'-style

The next three rugs (Plates 4–6) are anomalies in East Azarbayjan. They are alike in their use of strong color, as opposed to the more common undyed beige wool used in many rugs from East Azarbayjan, and all three have roughly similar structure. Although they appear to be from the same general area, only the first, Plate 4, can be localized with any degree of confidence. With their particular coloration they resemble Caucasian rugs to some extent. It is tempting to think an in-migration of weavers with different color sensibilities was responsible.

4

Size	3'6"–3'9" × 9'7" (114 × 292 cm)
Warp	Z2S ivory wool
Weft	Two singles, dark red, rose, ivory wool, two to four shots, plus dark blue selvedge reinforcement wool, up to 1" into the body of the rug
Knotting	V 8-9, H 9, 76.5/square inch, 1186/square dm; pile height about 4mm
Selvedges	Restored
Ends	Top: remnants of beige wool plainweave; Bottom: warp finish missing
Colors	10: dark blue, dark red, ivory, yellow, yellow orange, medium and dark green, light blue, aubergine, dark brown

'Qarajeh' long rug, *kennereh*

> *Qarajeh, field notes:* I'm looking on my dog-eared map for Karaja and pronounce it with the accent on the second syllable. Our guide and a contact from Tehran are mystified, as are the restaurant owners in Sarab who gave me the map. I point on the map to precisely where the village ought to be, and say 'Karaja' again, like a low-grade mynah bird. The guide smiles, and so do the restaurant owners, and they say, almost in chorus, 'G(Q)araJEH'. My first bit of field knowledge gained!

I visited Qarajeh twice. It is a small village with maybe 2,500 souls at the end of what was then a gravel road located in the dry upland area of East Azarbayjan, east of Tabriz, that is famous for production of intensely colored, single-wefted, cotton foundation export rugs and carpets. Pre-export boom, it was likely the source of wool foundation *kennereh* and *kelleh* format pile rugs (ca. 5' × 12') for local consumption, like this example. But the alleged output is rather high for a village of this size. There is not another in the immediate vicinity, and where else the style could have been sourced is unclear.[13] The villagers do not appear to have woven *sumak* articles but did weave *jajim*. They did now and then apparently weave pile khorjin, probably for sale in the bazaar, usually with dark blue fields and with single elements taken from *kennereh*.[14] They told me that they had had frequent contact with nomads in the past.

The borders here are fairly standard for such rugs and are similar to those from earlier times in 'Greater Azarbayjan' (includes the Transcaucasus), but the field exhibits strange and unusual large forms, some cloud collar-like, perhaps drawn from pre-Islamic times, others, palmette motifs that probably owe their existence to classical carpet design and Ottoman textiles. Usually, in rugs like this, the field elements are less varied. There is a jumble of small motifs, some of which may represent amulets or fetishes, that do not generally appear in export rugs from this village. They may represent relatively early weaving. Notable is the intense yellow in a field element.

As with a lot of older rugs, uneven warp tension was a problem here, which accounts for motifs not being perfectly straight.[15]

Small living room in a house in the village of Qarajeh, late summer, 1996, showing the common layout in the space: three *kennereh* with traditional motifs. The fabric-covered pillows and bolsters might at one time have been covered with locally woven textiles.

5

Size	3'5" × 6'11" (104 × 211 cm)
Warp	Z2S light beige wool
Weft	Two singles, beige to dark brown wool, two to three shots
Knotting	V 9, H 8, 72/square inch, 1116 per dm; pile height about 6mm; perhaps the beige pile in one medallion is camel-hair.
Selvedges	Disintegrated
Ends	Warp finishes missing
Colors	11: dark blue, ivory, red, abrashed green, light blue, undyed camel-hair (?), yellow orange, aubergine, red brown, yellow, dark brown

Azarbayjani (?) long rug

The field in this example contains the same general type of eight-pointed star as do many Qarajeh rugs (compare it with the yellow field element in Plate 4), albeit with the outer points sheared off by the border, and with similar wool type and coloration, but the rug is distinctly different. Camel-hair is seldom used for pile, as it is not durable, but it seems it provides the background for the bottom medallion in the field.

The design has a slightly melted quality about it, and the design units are familiar, but not in this combination. There is a rug in a similar design, cut down, in an American collection, but otherwise no comparable pieces come to mind. The guard borders are unusually wide, and the short format is also unusual.

There are two small motifs between the second and third medallions which may be devolved plant forms but look very much like ritual carvings of aurochs from, for example, predynastic Egypt. In any case, they appear in the same way in many East Azarbayjani pile weavings and seem to be an identifier for pile weaving from this area of Iran. The shrub forms between the first and second medallions are telltale Kurdish ornamentation. Many of the inhabitants of this area are said to be ethnic Kurds.

Although the piece is in more or less full pile, the edges and ends have disintegrated.

6

Size	2'8" × 6'2" (81 × 188 cm)
Warp	Z2S, Z3S mixed brown wool
Weft	Two singles, ivory to beige wool, two to three shots
Knotting	V 9, H 9, 81/square inch, 1256 per dm; pile height about 9mm
Selvedges	Two pairs of warps interlaced with pale beige wool
Ends	Top: Warp finish missing; Bottom: remnants of beige wool plainweave, terminating with remnants of warp loops
Colors	9: ivory, dark blue, dark yellow, rose, aubergine, brown red, green, light blue, dark brown

Azarbayjani (?) long rug

The salient aspect of this rug is the field design; the main border, with its emphasis on vertical and horizontal lines, is derived from slit-tapestry or other pile-less weaves. The relationship between the field design and a whole class of nineteenth century Shirvan/Dagestani prayer rugs is apparent, and they are probably rough contemporaries. However, the layout is less common in western Iran.

The origin of the ascending plants in the field is likely Kashmiri textiles woven with flower forms within a grid, but here with a Kurdish inflection. Although there is no grid here, it is simulated by the diagonally placed red and aubergine elements on the upper margins of each plant form. These forms impart a sense of motion.

The rug's dimensions are unusual for an old piece, as is the use of a single guard border. A good age indicator here is the presence of a good strong aubergine.

7

Size	3'2" × 8'11" (97 × 272 cm)
Warp	Z2S ivory wool, alternate warps slightly depressed
Weft	Two singles, light beige wool, two to three shots, some heavy brown/aubergine weft part way in from edge
Knotting	V 8–9, H 9, 72–84/square inch, 1186/square dm; pile height about 7 mm; knots densely packed.
Selvedges	Three pairs of reinforced warps interlaced with aubergine wool
Ends	One row aubergine wool 2/1 *sumak* warp end stopping followed by a chaining wrap, with the same material
Colors	8: beige, salmon, light blue, red, blue green, aubergine, ivory, dark brown

'Meshkin Shahr' long rug

This rug is a conundrum: It is dense, on a wool foundation, has high quality dyes used much as they were in the Transcaucasus, is precisely drawn, and with idiosyncratic color use. Pairs of not totally clear digits that could make up a four-digit date are separated by a field motif and are not knotted on the same level of wefts. They could be read with some effort as 1349/1930. Another set of contiguous numbers is illegible.

All the weaving's characteristics imply an earlier time of production than 1930. Regarding figuring out when rugs were woven, rural Azarbayjan in 1930 was a remote and isolated area, and quality rugs could have been woven then. But it just seems unlikely, if only because of the influx of synthetic dyes by that time.

This rug is a member of a small group with similar color and structure, right down to the *sumak* end stopping. It and others in this cluster have some mainstream Sarab-like motifs, so it is possible they come from a village near Sarab. It is also possible that they were the output of one small group of weavers located in any number of villages in East Azarbayjan. There's no easy way to know.

The rug does not have the typical Sarab layout of undecorated outer borders and predominately beige coloration, so could well have been woven by Transcaucasian or Kurdish migrants with a different color sensibility and be contemporary with old Sarab rugs.

By about 1900, color use and format had changed in some Sarab area villages that had previously woven mainly *kennereh* with beige wool. As Cecil Edwards writes, some weavers of narrow rugs were not producing what the market wanted. Relatively late long format Sarab rugs in general were denser, heavier, often narrower, and more regular in construction, possibly to meet external market demand. It has often been said that some of these come from Meshkin Shahr, a town directly north of the Sabalan massif, settled after about 1900 by nomads, but there is no hard documentation.

The particular hooked forms that surround the medallions in this rug (which repeat in the green medallion centers) are not generally seen in older Sarab-like weavings and there is some question as to where they originated. The aubergine dye in the guard border is slightly corroded, but the beige field color is not, and it is probably undyed wool. The main border is unusual for rugs from the area, with half medallions within a blue green and light blue serrated meander.

The original oblique interlaced bands that would have been warp finishes are missing. This can be inferred from similar rugs that have them.

Sarab

Sarab, at one time a town, now a small city with traffic lights, is on the western edge of a flat area in the south of East Azarbayjan, possibly a dry lake bed from earlier, wetter times. An Iranian who grew up in the area told of seeing nomads in the past come down to the town with their camels to trade with the local bazaaris.

One thinks of picture book 'Sarab' rugs as being long and narrow, with predominantly beige coloration, but woven with a variety of warp and weft material. Beige coloration predominates because villagers in East Azarbayjan have herds of mixed white, dark brown and beige sheep since they are not generally breeding white sheep for wool sale. It stands to reason that these villagers, who did not own camels because they did not migrate – that's what camels in this context were used for – wove rugs with 'camel' colored sheep's wool. Nomads had access to camel wool, but it is really seen quite rarely in rugs. Judging by the stability of design and use of natural dyes into the early twentieth century, there was less disturbance of local folkways for these weavers than for many other weaving communities. The next three rugs are typical of this genre (Plates 8–10).

The predilection for beige wool is also thought to reflect the Sarab weavers' Kurdish origins, even though these villagers speak Turkish. Richard Tapper, in private correspondence, wrote they are 'Turkicized' Kurds who probably arrived in this depopulated area in the late eighteenth century. The weavers of 'Sarab' rugs could have been forcibly moved from the Hamadan area to East Azarbayjan, or, possibly, could be descendants of local Shaqaqi Kurds.[16] The earliest dated (1231/1816) apparent 'Sarab' rug was published by Siawosch Azadi.[17]

Field notes: Obviously 9' × 12' carpets can fit into some village common rooms quite efficiently, and the three-runner approach to furnishing living space has a complex past, probably rooted in nomad narrow loom weaving conventions. In-country opinion is that *kennereh* were woven at one time on ground looms, but this approach might make it hard to weave a long *kennereh*. I have seen Sarab *kennereh* up to 28' long.

As we passed through the many small villages around Sarab, on the north side of the Bozgush, it seemed plausible to me that each might have been the source of a distinctive type of Sarab *kennereh* or *kelleh* in the nineteenth century, in pre-export times. This would be contrary to what I was told before, that is, that 'Sarab' rugs were woven over a fairly wide area of East Azarbayjan.

We wandered around in the town of Sarab a bit and saw a city-design carpet being woven with a *Herati* pattern in a Sehna weave. One rug shop had stacks of grim, very dull-looking, new Sarab *kennereh* for sale, so the story that *kennereh* weaving has died out here is not true. I asked an old Turki-speaking dealer in Sarab if the camel-colored pile in the typical new Sarab *kennereh* is dyed, and he said no, it is natural undyed wool from the area. Dye tests conducted for me on camel-colored wool in old Sarabs have come up negative. However, those pile rugs with corroded camel colored wool might be dyed or heavily washed.

8

Size	3'5" × 12'4" (104 × 376 cm)
Warp	Z2S beige wool, some ivory and brown interplied
Weft	Two singles, beige, occasionally ivory, wool, two shots
Knotting	V 7, H 7, 49/square inch, 760/square dm; pile height about 8 mm
Selvedges	Three pairs of reinforced warps interlaced with beige, greenish ivory and red wool
Ends	Top and bottom: three to five lines of beige wool plainweave
Colors	13: dark beige, rose red, dark green, ivory, dark blue, yellow, light blue, rose/salmon, dark red, pale grayish aubergine, pale beige, pale green, slightly corroded black

Sarab long rug, *kennereh*

Based on information from sources in Tabriz (for example, correspondence with Sa'id Ronaghian Tabrizi, who was giving what were probably earlier twentieth century impressions), beige colored 'Sarab' *kennereh* – long format pile rugs – typified by this piece, were woven not just in the town of Sarab and environs, but also in a series of villages such as Qarehchaman, halfway to Tabriz, Duzduzan, also to the west of Sarab, and Heris about 12 km south of Sarab (not the well-known carpet weaving village to the north). The variety of sources for these rugs probably accounts for the variability in warp and weft material.

Sarab rugs, woven primarily for a rural population in a format suitable for long narrow local houses,[18] are almost always without in-woven dates or inscriptions. This rug, on the other hand, has a clear, large, intact Islamic date of 1256 (1840). It is probably accurate because of the lack of a simplistic date composed of ones, twos and threes that in many cases was probably decorative. Dated folk art like this rug, whose weaving was likely not market-driven, is often commemorative. The very fact that it is not very different in color or format from Sarab *kennereh* from toward the end of the nineteenth century attests to the relative stability of the area over that time period. There was simply not the commercial pressure that caused the evolution of rug structure, colors and design in the Transcaucasus, parts of Iran and in Anatolia.

The plain or sparsely decorated wide outer border in Sarab *kennereh* is usually followed by two narrow interior borders. In this case, the rug is an outlier, because there are four in total. The one that is remarkable contains linked 'S' forms. The single row of medallions in the field, with their diagonal vestigial leaf forms, is a carryover from other weaving cultures.

That it has its original edges and ends makes this rug a valuable document.

۱۲۵۷

9

Size	3'6" × 10'4" (107 × 315 cm)
Warp	Z3S beige wool, alternate warps slightly depressed
Weft	Two singles, some Z2S, undyed cotton, one to five shots, some irregular
Knotting	V 8, H 9, 72/square inch, 1116/square dm; pile height about 7 mm
Selvedges	Two pairs of reinforced warps interlaced with beige and dark red wool
Ends	Top: remnants of rose wool plainweave: Bottom: Partially intact warp loops, followed by four lines of beige wool plainweave
Colors	9: beige, ivory, medium blue, abrashed red, yellow, dark blue, aubergine, salmon, uncorroded black

Related example: Burns, 2011, plate 9; Tschebull, 1995, plate 8
Published: Landreau, 1978, plate 46; Tschebull, 1995, plate 7

Sarab long rug, *kennereh*

The field combines the common Islamic design concepts of pendant medallions, here repeated one and two thirds times, and an endless repeat, evidenced by half and quarter medallions at the margins of the field. Despite the lack of symmetry, which might imply a late date, this is quite an old rug, based on the number and quality of dyes, the complex design, and the irregular weave. Atypically, there is a non-corrosive black, an intense red, deep aubergine, and a saturated yellow. The beige pile is likely undyed. There is a comparable rug, in the Burns collection, with the same field design concept, secondary border and similar colors, but reduced on four sides.

The diamond grid containing vestigial flowering plants in the beige field of rugs like this seems to echo Kashmiri textile influence; there is no other logical source. Assuming this theory on design origin is correct, it is another example of how widely design concepts can travel.

But most of the rest of the design elements in this rug are closely related to pre-export long rugs from the Hamadan area, said in conversation with Siawosch Azadi to have been woven by the Qaragöz, semi-nomads who lived west of that city. The similarities can include: tone on tone beige pile, undecorated or sparsely decorated outside borders, and those repeat pendant medallions. The pendant medallion design that appears as a single row in Sarab *kennereh* repeats horizontally in wider carpets from the Hamadan area. Major differences are that the Hamadan-area rugs are more finely knotted, with shorter pile and on cotton foundations. A few of these have in-woven dates from the early nineteenth century. It appears that the Qaragöz style persisted longer in East Azarbayjan than in Hamadan, where, after about 1900, they began to weave market-oriented rugs and carpets with more color and a variety of designs that were aimed at Western customers.

The red medallion centers in this rug are derived from '*Mina Khani*' forms, which were used in western Iran, most prominently in alleged 'Sangor' Kurdish rugs, from southern Iranian Kurdistan. The *Mina Khani* design is commonly seen on Turkmen pile-woven transport bags and in Khorasani 'Baluch' carpets and bags. There may be an intermediate stage somewhere, between the Turkmen *Mina Khani* design and the red Sarab motif. Does it perhaps have an origin in Safavid or Ottoman court design?

10

Size	5'1" × 11'2" (155 × 340 cm)
Warp	Z4S undyed cotton, alternate warps slightly depressed
Weft	Two singles, undyed cotton, salmon cotton(?), dark brown wool, two shots
Knotting	V 11, H 6.5, 71.5/square inch, 1108/square dm; pile height about 10mm
Selvedges	Two pairs of reinforced warps interlaced with beige wool
Ends	Warp finishes missing
Colors	10: beige, ivory, blue green, red, aubergine, medium blue, yellow, dark blue, rose, black

Published: Tschebull, 1995, plate 5

Sarab carpet, *kelleh*

On cold winter nights, villagers would want to sit on a heavy rug like this. It weighs 32.5 pounds (14.77kg), which is as heavy as a room-sized 'Heriz' export carpet from the same general area. Tabriz bazaaris, who controlled the export rug trade in relatively nearby environs like Sarab, were well known for skimping on wool for rug production, but this rug was produced in a structure more typical for the internal market.

The design elements in this rug are similar to those in Plate 9. The ivory medallions, which have the vague shape and a quartered layout like Turkmen guls, reflect the durability of ancient tribal designs. The inner border is a local version of a common meander, but with Kurdish-style leaves alternating with stepped diamond-like forms substituting for the usual stylized palmettes; the outer large green and aubergine reciprocal border looks as if it was mosaic felt or slit-tapestry *kilim*-inspired.

The Z4S warps in the foundation might have been commercially sourced, as multi-ply warps are a marker for urban weaving. There are other rugs with similar drawing and coloration, just not very many. The format is exactly that of nomad *kilims* from the same area and is likely a carryover from a nomad tradition.

The 'horned beasts' similar to those in other rugs from the same area (see Plates 5, 11) appear in the undecorated right outer border.

11

Size	3'5" × 7'2" (104 × 218 cm)
Warp	Z3S ivory wool, alternate warps slightly depressed
Weft	Two singles, ivory wool, two shots
Knotting	V 11, H 9, 99/square inch, 1535/square dm; pile height about 5mm
Selvedges	None
Ends	Warp finishes missing, ends reduced
Colors	9: dark blue, yellow, ivory, red, green, medium blue, undyed beige, ivory, uncorroded dark brown

Published: Tschebull, 1995, plate 6

'Sarab' long rug

This rug and the three that follow (Plates 11–14) are hard to localize, because there are not many – or any, in some cases – similar pieces, which might give a basis for assignment to areas or villages. They are examples of how hard it is to figure out where many East Azarbayjani village rugs were woven.

All the typical Sarab pile rug motifs – the *Mina Khani*-derived medallions, the diamond-shaped grid, a version of the border seen in Plate 10, and even two horned beasts – appear in this rug, but the saturated colors are what one would tend to see in Transcaucasian pile rugs or Azarbayjani nomad *sumak* bags and *jajims*, and the motifs themselves are drawn differently from typical Sarab rugs. The rug's structure is more typically Transcaucasian. It is a pity there are no selvedges or end finishes to help with identification.

The use of a yellow background border and a dark blue field echoes coloration in repeat *Mina Khani* design *kennereh* allegedly woven near Sangor, west of Hamadan in southern Kurdistan,[19] and may be a carryover, a memory, brought with Kurdish migrants from that general area who moved north into East Azarbayjan. It is quite possible the style was altered post-migration and retained the color relationships; the complete 'Sangor' design is not common in rural East Azarbayjani weaving. This is all informed speculation.

The red *Mina Khani* forms in the straight-sided ivory medallions are almost unrecognizable as Sarab elements, as are the plant forms in the grid. There is a hint of a repeat medallion design in the elements in the blue field where there is no grid.

The borders are flanked by 'barber's-pole' guards, in the Caucasian style. As opposed to the idea of its having been woven by descendants of Kurdish migrants, was this rug perhaps woven near Sarab by villagers of another ethnicity, either settled nomads originally from the Transcaucasus, or much less likely, by nomads in a winter camp? There are very few rugs like this, so comparisons cannot be readily made.

12

Size	3'5" × 11'4" (104 × 345 cm)
Warp	Z3S undyed cotton
Weft	Two singles, undyed cotton, two shots
Knotting	V 11 H 9, 99/square inch, 1535/square dm; pile height about 4mm
Selvedges	None
Ends	Top: Partial oblique interlaced band of warp material; Bottom: Warp finish missing
Colors	7: ivory, orange, green, light blue, salmon, dark blue, uncorroded brown/black.

Published: Landreau et al., 1978, plate 47;
Tschebull, 1995, plate 11

'Sarab' long rug, *kennereh*

There are a few Kurdish rugs in this design, but other Sarab-like pieces similar to this example and the next (Plate 13) are very rare. Scarcity speaks to age and/or small populations that did the weaving.

Layers of pendant medallions within pendant medallions and the grid-less floral repeat on ivory make the origin of the design clear, as do the *Mina Khani* motif and the not very precisely drawn 'Qarajeh-style' eight-pointed stars in the medallion centers. But as with Plate 11, there is no undecorated outside border, and the endless repeat can only be seen in the dark blue indents, which imply half and quarter pendant medallions. The infilling in those indents is with elements that often appear in *sumak* bags.

The stepped motif in the discontinuous main border at the bottom of the rug derives from warp-substitution weaves, primarily pack-bands and *jajims* used by Azarbayjani nomads. The weavers of this *kennereh* might have been settled nomads, but the interchange of designs between villagers and nomads was likely not very rigid, so trying to make hard determinations about village vs. nomad design sources is often not particularly useful.

The weave is fairly dense. The all-cotton foundation is somewhat of an anomaly, but so is the rug itself.

13

Size	3'3" × 12'10" (99 × 391 cm)
Warp	Z3S, 2 wool, 1 undyed cotton interplied
Weft	Two singles, undyed cotton, two shots
Knotting	V 10 H 7.5, 75/square inch, 1163/square dm; pile height about 4mm
Selvedges	None
Ends	Top: Oblique interlaced band of warp material; Bottom: Warp finish missing
Colors	10: ivory, dark blue, pale brown red, dark brown/black, medium blue, red, blue green, yellow, pale salmon, undyed beige camel-hair

Published: Tschebull, 1995, plate 12

'Sarab' long rug, *kennereh*

Bought in midsummer at 10 pm on a London back street along with the previous rug, Plate 12, presumably from the same former owner once removed, this piece must have come from the same weavers, in or near East Azarbayjan, as its companion, since many of the colors and most of the design elements are similar. However, there are substantial differences: this rug is more pliable, partially due to the composition of the warp; there are more colors; fewer nomad-like design elements, and the pendant medallion concept is much closer to the Sarab archetype. It just goes to show that weavings produced almost surely by the same weavers at the same time can vary quite a bit.

Coloration in these two *kennereh*, as too with Plate 11, is reversed from the Sarab norm, with a dark pendant medallion on a light field.

Why interply wool and cotton for warp material? It was done elsewhere occasionally in Azarbayjan and may have only had to do with what material was available.

14

Size	3'5" × 14'0" (104 × 427 cm)
Warp	Z3S beige wool
Weft	Two singles, beige and orange wool, one shot
Knotting	V 11, H 8, 88/square inch, 1408/square dm; pile height about 5mm
Selvedges	Two pairs of reinforced warps interlaced with dark brown/black wool
Ends	Top: Oblique interlaced band of warp material; Bottom: remnants of 13 mm beige wool plainweave with most warps ending in loops.
Colors	7: ivory, orange, green, light blue, salmon, dark blue, uncorroded brown/black. There is a dark ink stain in the border.

Azarbayjani long rug, *kennereh*

Occasionally, *kennereh* were woven in Azarbayjan that exhibited single rows of Turkmen ornaments in various styles, but rarely the '*Dyrnak*' gul, as here. It is reasonable to assume these rugs were woven by Turkmen remnant populations.

As opposed to the original Turkmen design, the guls in this *kennereh* have been reordered onto a central pole and had their interiors changed, but the half and quarter medallions at the field margins imply an endless repeat, much as in an old Turkmen rug. But there is a lightness of being versus the Turkmen model, with the field changed from red to ivory, more green and light blue introduced, and almost no dark blue. The design is basic and repetitive, but the color usage in all the elements changes subtly, so the overall impression is not one of stiffness.

It has been opined by an Azarbayjani that this rug is from the pre-commercial period, woven in Heriz. In support of this, the single weft shots and coloration are much like that seen in presumably later export carpets. If the rug was used domestically in Iran, it probably had considerably longer pile, as it would have been used to sit on. Often, old long pile rugs from Iran are sheared in the West to make the designs clearer and thus make them more marketable.

Export Rugs

Drawing on the color sensibility, design concepts, and weaving skills that make Azarbayjani nomad and village weaving for domestic use so attractive, East Azarbaijani weavers produced smaller pieces in the export tradition that can be as compelling examples of textile art as any similar sized Turkish or Caucasian rug.

This next four smallish export rugs (Plates 15–18) are quite different, one from the other. They are arranged in rough order of their distance from village weaving for domestic use and display different aspects of export rug design. This group is most interesting as these weavings are cultural hybrids of a sort, reflecting a clear combination of Western and domestic styles and formats.

15

Size	4'5" × 8'0" (135 × 244 cm)
Warp	Z5S undyed cotton, alternate warps slightly depressed
Weft	Two singles, undyed cotton, random beige, light blue and red wool, two-three shots
Knotting	V 9, H 7.5, 67.5/square inch, 1046/square dm; pile height about 4mm
Selvedges	One pair of reinforced warps interlaced with light and dark beige wool
Ends	Warp finishes missing
Colors	9: abrashed medium/light blue, beige, ivory, soft red, dark aubergine, blue green, yellow, rose, brown/black

Related example: Herrmann, 1983, Plate 49

'Sarab' rug

The use of light blue and beige and an undecorated outside border may be Kurdish traditions adapted to export weaving in East Azarbayjan, and the look of this piece is distinctly like what one would see in 'Bijar' rugs. The color combination is often seen in large Azarbayjani carpets, sometimes with pendant medallion designs, as in this example, but is not at all common in rugs woven for domestic consumption.

The general impression of those who know rugs from East Azarbayjan is that beige and light blue were used in some of the earlier (late nineteenth century) export rugs and carpets, sourced in the larger towns like Bakshaish and Sarab. Erberhart Herrmann has noted the beige/blue color combination in cotton foundation rugs and carpets and cites Ulrich Schürmann, who estimated that a similar colored rug could be dated to 1800. But this appears to be an optimistic guess. As usual, there is no hard evidence, and commercial reality is that large cotton foundation carpets from this area were usually destined for an export market that developed late in the nineteenth century.

This example may be from Sarab, because of the denser knotting than is seen in weavings normally ascribed to Bakshaish and the undecorated outer border, but there is no sure attribution. The structure is less dense than in a typical export 'Heriz'.

The border, uncommon, features an 'S' motif seen in Kurdish pile rugs, and is probably taken from dragon rug borders that were woven two hundred years earlier, perhaps in East Azarbayjan.

'Lazy lines' and discontinuous wefts indicate the rug may have been woven by three women. There are places where extra wefts have been added to make the rug lie flat or to correct a curvature.

16

Size	4'8" × 6'6" (142 × 198 cm)
Warp	Z4S undyed cotton, alternate warps depressed
Weft	Two singles, undyed cotton, random beige, one (?) shot
Knotting	V 10, H 7, 70/square inch, 1085/square dm; pile height about 4mm
Selvedges	Two pairs of reinforced warps interlaced with 1" to 3" segments of wool in all the colors used for pile
Ends	Warp finishes missing, end borders slightly reduced
Colors	8: orange red, blue green, very dark blue, salmon, yellow, medium to light blue, ivory, light green

'Heriz' rug

Azarbayjani rugs in this dimension were not common until the beginning of the twentieth century and may have been simply formatted to compete with other bold squarish rugs, like Caucasian Kazaks. These 'Heriz' rugs, named after one of the larger weaving villages that is known for high quality export rugs and carpets, come from a variety of towns and villages in East Azarbayjan, including Mehreban, Bakshaish, Sarab, Sarabian and smaller settlements whose names are unknown at this point.

Good ones are sought after because the almost square format works well with the traditional 'Heriz' medallion and spandrels design. The rugs themselves are dense and durable and have survived in some numbers. But they can be ruined with a bit of abuse. Slicker versions were almost certainly sourced from Tabriz area workshops, as were so-called silk Herizes.

There is a tendency to overdate this group of rugs and carpets. Most are from post 1900, based on acquisition data. Village dyers in East Azarbayjan were producing high quality natural dyes on hand-spun wool into the late 1920s and sometimes beyond. It should be noted that these dyers each produced a slightly different madder red, and 'Heriz' export carpets can be grouped on the basis of that hue. Hand spun wool was common up until about 1950.

This example is out of the ordinary because of its coloration, especially its very dark blue which has a black value; its 'animal pelt' design, which might have zoomorphic origins, as well as its unusual borders, especially the main one on dark blue, with its free form palmettes. From field experience, weavers often use samplers for borders, but maybe not for this main border. Only the outside guard border is seen in other rugs of this type, at least in my experience.

Because these rugs were woven for the export market, dealers often specified what should be woven, sometimes even supplying the dyed yarn. But really good weavers called their own shots, wove what they wanted and had dealers lined up to buy their wares. In almost any weaving village, the best weaver was easy to find, and still is. This rug is probably the product of just such a weaver.[20]

An older weaver's Heriz carpet border sampler and her weaving tools on the bench in front of her loom. The relatively old sampler is woven with hand-spun wool and probably natural dyes. There were objects like this in village houses I visited but, being a guest, I never tried to buy anything.

17

Size	5'10" × 7'3" (178 × 221 cm)
Warp	Z3S mixed beige, ivory and brown wool, alternate warps slightly depressed
Weft	Two mixed wool and cotton singles, some Z2S, ivory, beige, brown, 1–2 shots
Knotting	V 9, H 11, 99/square inch, 1535/square dm; pile height about 5mm
Selvedges	Two pairs of reinforced warps interlaced with beige wool
Ends	Warp finishes missing, top narrow red border missing
Colors	10: medium blue, red, pale yellow, rose (variable), blue green, light blue, aubergine, ivory, undyed beige, brown/black

fig. 1 Bakshaish *Bid Majnun* design carpet (detail). Author's collection.

'Bakshaish' carpet

This rug, with an unusual field pattern, is one of a cluster, many having a garden design called *Bid Majnun* in Farsi, with stylized but recognizable cypresses, weeping willows and cynar trees.[21] The *Bid Majnun* design also appears on a fragment in my collection which has the same colors as this rug (*fig.1*).

Some extraordinary examples in the group of which this is a member have landscape designs that hark back to Mongol miniatures. Regardless of design, almost all are approximately 5'6" × 7'0"/168 × 210 cm, which is a format most appealing to the export market, so it is reasonable to assume that that is why they were woven. Virtually all have similar structure: knot count on average, ca. 100 kpsi (1550 k/dm²); ivory/beige wool warps, alternate warps slightly depressed; wefts mostly cotton, but also mixed cotton and wool and sometimes all wool. The group is described as having been woven in Bakshaish, but there is no hard evidence for this.

fig. 1

They are characterized by the frequent use of a medium to light blue for field color and a red background main border (rarely dark brown/black) which is a corrupted meander and leaf design, derived from a Kurdish border which may be older. The drawing in these 'Bakshaish' rug borders is somewhat variable from one rug to another, but almost always with the same main elements and secondary colors, while field designs are often more precisely executed. A cartoon may have been used just for the field.

The red, rose and aubergine club-like vertical forms in the field of the pictured rug are probably derived from remarkably similar elements on each side of the repeat palmettes in Caucasian 'shield' carpets.[22] The motif, looking like a lily in profile, may be ultimately passed down from Mughal/Safavid floral carpet designs and/or embroideries. The entire field design was sometimes used in large carpets woven for export, probably from Tabriz.

There are rugs in this group with Bid Majnun fields on dark blue within a prayer rug design and with red background rosette/meander borders, but generally too big to be real prayer rugs.[23] In any case, the concept of a prayer rug is foreign to the Shia Muslims who inhabit northwestern Iran, and they are hardly ever seen in village/folk art weaving.

The 'horned beasts' that appear randomly in various colors in field ornaments (see also Plates 5, 11), plus the use of undyed beige wool for highlights, are pretty sure Azarbayjani indicators.

18

Size	5'6" × 9'11" (168 × 302 cm)
Warp	Z4S undyed cotton, alternate warps depressed
Weft	Two cotton singles, one undyed, one thinner, dyed light blue, 2 shots
Knotting	V 7, H 7, 49/square inch, 760/square dm; pile height about 4mm
Selvedges	Two pairs of reinforced warps interlaced with red brown wool
Ends	Warp finishes missing
Colors	9: red, dark blue, abrashed light blue, yellow, blue green, ivory, aubergine, rose, dark yellow/beige

'Tabriz' carpet

Rugs that are a bit mysterious can have a compelling draw. The rug looks a bit like a sampler but seems too large to have served that purpose efficiently. The central design unit seems freeform, but is actually repeated, taking up about forty percent of the field at the beginning of the rug, is then flipped, and flipped again, almost to complete the design, a third time. As the design is complex, it was almost certainly woven from a cartoon; this technique of flipping designs is fairly common in large workshop carpets.

In addition to its city workshop characteristics, the rug has village weaving aspects. The strong coloration, a random small animal, the border style and the low knot density are what one would expect to find in rugs and carpets from the towns east of Tabriz, and the format is not usual for an Azarbayjani export rug.

But many Heriz-like rugs and carpets like this one were woven in workshops in or near the city of Tabriz, in East Azarbayjan. They usually have slightly different selvedge treatment and less wool is used in the weaving process, as compared with village work.

19

Size	4'10" × 10'6" (147 × 320 cm)
Warp	Z3S ivory wool; a few warps 2ZS ivory, some dark brown wool interplied, 9 per inch, 23 per dm
Weft	Two wool singles, 18 ± per inch, 46 per dm, using the slit-tapestry technique
Selvedges	Bundle of three warps reinforced with aubergine and beige wool
Ends	Warp finishes missing
Colors	5: red, aubergine, rose/pink, medium blue, beige (probably dyed)

Exhibited: MFA, Boston, 2014–15[24]

Azarbayjani tapestry-weave gilim

Long Azarbayjani *gilim* – the Iranian transliteration of the more common Turkish *kilim* – with plain fields may have been woven for use as *sofreh*,[25] and indeed, this piece has what look like faint food stains along the center (see similar discussion, Plate 3). The weavers here worked with a very limited palette, yet knew precisely how to combine their colors, which implies that they had woven this pattern before; yet there are apparently no other published examples just like it.

Where the irregular zig-zag elements meet, the tapestry weaving technique causes each return weft to step up one warp diagonally, producing an interface that virtually eliminates the structural weakness inherent in much slit-tapestry weaving. It is surprising it was not used more often in East Azarbayjan.

Some similar *gilims* have a single line of wrapped outlines along the warps where the colors meet, which hides the slightly exposed warps. The disadvantage is that it often wears off with use.

This *gilim* has restrained eccentric wefts but lies perfectly flat. The colors are not flat in appearance, to some extent because of the slight variation in the dyes but also due to uneven weft density and the variable spin and diameter of the yarn. This combination makes the *gilim* 'dance'. There are a few simple brocaded design elements, some of which are partially worn away. It was fairly recently collected in Jolfa, in northern East Azarbayjan, and has colors typical of Azarbayjani village weaving, especially the rose/pink color (called 'cooked shrimp' by rug restoration expert Bob Mann). But the fact that it has a wool warp may indicate it is nomad work. The format, from my field observation of similar pieces in use by Azarbayjani nomads, is typical as ground cover in a yurt.

The design concept is fairly common in Afshar *sofrehs*, and there is a version of it in Fars *gilims*.[26] The serrated elements may have some symbolic meaning.[27]

It seems counterproductive to try to fix a date of production for weavings like this, especially in a vacuum, but there are *gilims* from Azarbayjan in the same format woven with similar color and material with fairly clear in-woven dates from between 1885 and 1905.[28] It seems reasonable to date this *gilim* to the same period. The fact that high quality nomad *gilims* were being woven around the beginning of the twentieth century, should help to reduce some of the date snobbism that exists.[29] In general, flatweaves' lack of durability would tend to militate toward younger rather than older.

Jajims

Production of warp-faced fabric probably dates well back into Neolithic times. An early hint of long lineage is a 5,000-year-old silver proto-Elamite man/bull wearing a vertically striped 'tuning-fork' patterned cloak.[30] Warp-faced fabric would not fall right if worn with the stripes oriented horizontally.

Joseph in *Genesis* may well have worn a striped warp-faced garment – it is often so imagined and is depicted as such in illustrations. And there are tomb murals at Beni Hasan in Upper Egypt from about 1900 BCE that tend to confirm for biblical scholars what Joseph wore. A similar textile used as a blanket is in a fourteenth century Iranian miniature,[31] and *jajims* appear as camel covers in Qajar paintings.

There is carryover into nineteenth century nomad and village weaving in Iran and the Transcaucasus in the next eight textiles (Plates 20–27) in the form of *jajims*, used as felt-backed seating, quilt tops, for animal covers, and as bedding decoration.[32]

Complete *jajims* have approximately 1"/2.5 cm hems at each end to secure them. Most do not have selvedges, but rather, simple weft returns; some have sewn on decorative selvedges.

Transcaucasian *jajim* sewn onto a white felt backing, shown at the First Carpet Exhibition held in 1926 in Quba. Photograph by A. Alekbarov. Courtesy Togrul Efendiev/ Azerbaijan National Carpet Museum Archive, Baku.

20

Size	6'0" × 9'0" (183 × 274 cm)
Warp	Z2S tightly plied wool; 56 per inch, 142 per dm
Weft	Brown/beige wool singles, 16 per inch, 41 per dm
Selvedges	Weft returns
Ends	Original hems with brown and ivory wool
Joins	Fine wool 'cretan' stitch in 2"–4" segments, using all the warp colors, joining five panels
Colors	5: red, green, dark brown/black, medium blue, ivory

Azarbayjani nomad (?) warp-faced jajim

As good dyes are expensive, *jajims* with colors as intense as in this piece are a testament to the importance of this type of textile to Azarbayjani nomads and villagers. A further indication of its value to its original owners is its fine weave and the way the joins were sewn in with great care. Given the large size it is likely that this *jajim* was intended to be a camel cover or to cover stacked-up bedding in a house, but its very good condition indicates it was laid back and hardly ever used. I have seen old *jajims* like this one, woven by a distant ancestor, kept in village houses.

There are other Azarbayjani *jajims* with the same color and pattern combination, so it could be attributed to a fairly large tribal group, possibly Shahsavan who summered on Mount Sabalan.[33]

Jajims were woven on a ground loom as a continuous long strip, using a movable heddle, and were cut into lengths appropriate for the size of the cover desired, demonstrating modular construction at its most practical.

21

Size	6'2" × 5'7" (188 × 170 cm)
Warp	Z2S tightly plied wool; 48 per inch, 122 per dm
Weft	Red and medium blue wool singles, 16 per inch, 41 per dm
Selvedges	Weft returns, with ¾"/2 cm finger woven wool black and ivory warp-faced diamond-patterned surround sewn onto three sides
Ends	Top: original hem with red wool Bottom: hemmed, possibly not original
Joins	Simple overcasting stitch in red wool, joining four panels and the surround
Colors	6: red, pale yellow, medium blue, peach, green, dark brown/black

Azarbayjani nomad (?) warp-faced jajim

This is a somewhat fragile piece because the wefts are not packed down tightly, but the slightly exposed wefts create the effect of tinting the warp colors a bit, producing marginally altered hues. Half of the left-hand panel is wefted with medium blue, and it subtly contrasts with the rest of the *jajim*.

Square *jajims* like this were usually felt-backed and used to sit on in a yurt. Safavid miniatures show this tradition of sitting on apparently warp-faced padded woven fabric has a long history.

There are photographs from the mid-sixties by the anthropologist Richard Tapper showing *jajims* and other flatweaves with dyed red felt backing being loaded onto camels. Sometimes felt-backed *jajims* turn up in the Istanbul market and there is one in the Carpet Museum in Baku, but the norm in the trade is to remove the backing.

This textile may be slightly shortened, but there is no way to tell. The right-hand panel was flipped, so that the color sequence, left to right, is broken, and the effect is quite artful.

The weave, the coloration and the black and ivory woven surround make this *jajim* a bit of an outlier, so it is difficult to know where in northwest Iran it comes from. Although it was purchased in Iran, it could possibly be Transcaucasian.

22

Size	6'5" × 6'6" (196 × 198 cm)
Warp	Z2S tightly plied wool; 48 per inch, 122 per dm
Weft	Dark brown wool singles, 12 per inch, 30 per dm
Selvedges	weft returns
Ends	Original hems with brown wool
Joins	Simple overcasting stitch in aubergine and dark brown wool joining eight panels
Colors	8: red, brown/aubergine, dark brown, medium blue, dark blue, blue green, ivory, yellow

Azarbayjani (?) nomad warp-substitution-weave jajim

It is said that warp-substitution *jajim* were among the most difficult textiles to weave,[34] and they appear to be a Transcaucasian/Azarbayjani nomad speciality. Also, they tend to have more color variety than most plain *jajim*. In the case of this *jajim*, which is made up from one strip more than fifty feet long, maintaining the warp tension must have been a chore. The high warp count makes the small designs quite clear, even though they do not reproduce well in a full view plate.

The designs here form no pattern and seem to be the equivalent of weavers' doodles. There is all manner of small devices, including weavers' combs, comb animals and dragons (at least according to Iranians with extensive experience with dragons) in a large number of saturated colors. Some of these motifs tend to make appearances in guard borders in Caucasian and Azarbayjani pile rugs and may be carryovers from prehistoric times when bands and mats were woven with bast fiber.

The pattern warps that trail on the back of the piece between designs add padding to what is essentially a seating mat and serve to augment felt backing; this floating warp characteristic may account for the number of warp-substitution *jajim* in this format.

Parviz Tanavoli illustrates a similar piece in black and white and attributes it to the Saveh area.[35] But without any information as to where this piece was collected, it is difficult to know precisely where it was woven.

23

Size	5'7" × 6'7" (170 × 201 cm)
Warp	Z2S tightly plied wool; 64 per inch, 163 per dm
Weft	Dark brown wool singles, 16 per inch, 41 per dm
Selvedges	weft returns, with ¾"/2 cm finger woven black surround attached to four sides
Ends	Original hems with brown wool
Joins	Simple overcasting stitch in dark brown wool joining nine panels
Colors	8: red, blue green, dark blue, red brown, ivory, aubergine, dark brown, salmon

Azarbayjani (?) nomad warp-substitution-weave jajim

Pack bands used by nomads to secure loads while migrating share some motifs with warp-substitution *jajims*, in this case, a meander with half medallions, or 'flying birds' if the negative space is viewed differently. The design interruption in the eighth panel to the right did not occur because of a lack of weaving skill, but there is no ready explanation for it.

This *jajim* is made up of two separately woven panels of slightly different widths, that on the loom were 26'–33' long, one with red plainweave and a dark blue patterned section, the other, blue green plainweave and dark red patterning. The variation in width is probably intentional, to produce some variety in design, and occurs in many similar *jajims*. A salmon and dark brown narrow diamond border in the blue green/dark red panel appears in Uzbek warp-faced bands.

Warp-substitution *jajims* can have higher warp counts as well as more colors than most of those that are simply warp-faced, and this may reflect some sort of hierarchy of use.

The dark brown surround attached to this piece is not commonly seen in Azarbayjani *jajims*. While this example is probably from the Sabalan area, it may well be from the Transcaucasus, as this type of surround is seen attached to what are apparently Transcaucasian *jajims*.

This elaborate textile has at least three madder dyes, which is typical for older pile rugs from the nearby villages, where dye technology was advanced. It seems likely that the dye source for the nomads was also the village dyers. Every small weaving town had at least one.

24

Size	6'4" × 6'10" (193 × 208 cm)
Warp	Z2S tightly plied wool, 56 per inch, 142 per dm
Weft	Dark brown wool singles, 16 per inch, 41 per dm
Selvedges	Weft returns
Ends	Original hems with light brown wool; two panels hemmed in 2"/5 cm at one end
Joins	Simple overcasting stitch in light brown wool joining eleven panels
Colors	7: medium blue, brown red, orange red, ivory, yellow, brown/black, green

Azarbayjani (?) nomad warp-substitution-weave jajim

The design in this *jajim* was apparently fairly widely used in several areas in East Azarbayjan and perhaps in the Transcaucasus. There is a version that has the saturated colors as in Moghan/Sabalan bags and *jajim*, but here the colors are more muted, the fabric is heavier weight, and the wool is dryer. It is perhaps from as far south as Saveh, which Parviz Tanavoli also thinks is possible. There is no acquisition data other than its previous owner bought it in Iran.

Within the decorated panels, the warp-substitution motif of half medallions within a meander may be the vector for a large number of pile rug border designs used on village and workshop looms (see Plate 7, 'Meshkin Shahr', and Plate 32, 'Borjalu Kazak'). The motif appears almost exactly in the border of a woman's garment in an early thirteenth century polychromed German carving of *The Visitation*.[36]

The yellow design panels are narrower than the ivory ones, but some of the latter differ in width among themselves, probably due to uneven warp tension. The dark brown and ivory guard borders are quite variable, and exhibit what are said to be dragon forms as well as 'tuning fork'/humanoids.

The right-hand panel contains one large animal that has an upturned tail and probably represents a dog. Dogs were and are important members of the family for Azarbayjani nomads, as guards against both wolves and unwelcome visitors. The human form on the right, with long fingers and toes, is rare but not unique, and is reproduced in at least one other similar *jajim*. *Jajim* weaving was a conservative imitative art form and duplicates are to be expected. Warp-substitution weaving has not been commonly practiced by nomads in Azarbayjan for quite some time.

Big, short-tempered dogs, chained for our benefit, in front of felt-covered *kumes* in a Moghanlu camp at about 2,000 meters elevation.

25

Size	5'0" × 6'0" (152 × 183 cm)
Warp	Z2S tightly plied wool, 64 per inch, 163 per dm
Weft	Dark brown wool singles, 16 per inch, 41 per dm
Selvedges	Weft returns, with ½"/1.5 cm finger woven dark brown/black surround sewn onto four sides
Ends	Original hems with medium blue wool
Joins	Simple dense overcasting stitch in medium blue wool joining six panels
Colors	8: red brown, teal blue, red, medium blue, ivory, yellow, brown/black, green

Transcaucasian (?) nomad warp-substitution-weave jajim

Normally, a warp-substitution *jajim* with contrasting panels would be made up from two separate weavings cut to length and sewn together in alternating colors. It works fine for larger *jajims*, but in this case, it is apparent that a smaller format for the end product was desired, and that smaller ornaments might look better. Reduced scale made it possible to weave two designs in one strip. Ornament order varies between the panels, so there is no rigid progression.[37]

This design, '*yaddi qardash*' in Turki,[38] is reputed to be the most difficult among warp-substitution *jajim* patterns to weave because of its complexity, and it appears in both Transcaucasian and Azarbayjani *jajims*. The same combination of ornaments is, for the most part, used together. Because of its complexity, it may have been a carefully learned pattern.[39]

As there are examples of this type of *jajim* in the Carpet Museum in Baku, establishing that the design was woven in the Transcaucasus, it is possible the design spread across the Aras River into Azarbayjan with migrating nomads, whether they were fleeing political situations or simply seeking new pastures.

One unpublished fragment of a Transcaucasian warp-substitution horse cover contains large 'S' forms that look related to the '*yaddi qardash*' design. Both that fragment and this *jajim* have plain stripes of a slightly bluish red. The color, without chemical analysis, appears to be to be cooler than most madder tones, but is not in the range of normal cochineal dyes. Several warp-substitution *jajims* with similar designs have almost identical red tones in their plainweave stripes, which raises the question of a possible dye source.

The tentative attribution of this *jajim* to the Transcaucasus is based on similar weavings bought in the Caucasus and the use of a dark brown braided surround, which does not seem to be a common feature in Azarbayjani *jajims*.

26

Size	5'0" × 5'4" (152 × 163 cm)
Warp	Z2S tightly plied wool, 50 per inch, 127 per dm
Weft	Dark brown wool singles, 14 per inch, 36 per dm
Selvedges	weft returns
Ends	Top: Original hems with beige wool Bottom: 8–9"/20–23 cm narrow braided warps, tied off with narrow bands of contrasting colored wool
Joins	Simple overcasting stitch in beige wool joining the two outer panels; center join, 'cretan' stitch joining the two inner panels in ½"/1.5 cm segments with colors used in the warp
Colors	7: red, teal, dark blue, dark brown, green, ivory, salmon

Transcaucasian warp-faced jajim horse cover (?)

Is this textile a horse cover? It came from Baku relatively recently, described as '*terekeme*', a term derived from Arabic and used by academics in Baku to describe Transcaucasian nomads, but there are no straps to attach it to any animal, nor are there any signs of them. But the format and the one braided warp end make it seem likely it was intended to be an animal cover, even though it does not have the ear-like extensions normally seen on Transcaucasian/Azarbayjani horse covers. It does not appear to be a type of weaving normally attributed to Northwestern Iran.

The weaver has constructed this cover from two separate strips, and used four panels in total, with two flipped for symmetry, each almost twice as wide as usual. Normally, a *jajim* like this would have been composed of a larger number of panels, with seams almost unnoticeable between color blocks and the very narrow stripes. To preserve symmetry/balance with the wide dark blue-colored stripes, the weaver in this case has had to construct a join down the middle of the teal stripes, which she did quite well. The decoration is fairly severe, minimalist even, consisting of two lines of twining near the bottom of the piece, the elaborate braids, and the carefully worked multicolored 'cretan' stitches down the middle.

Given its pristine condition, it likely was never finished for use, and was put aside as capital. It is remarkable that, after all these years, textiles like this are still coming out of the Transcaucasus.

27

Size	3'4" × 4'3" (102 × 130 cm)
Warp	Z2S silk, 84 per inch, 213 per dm
Weft	Brown silk singles, 32 per inch, 81 per dm
Selvedges	Weft returns over a pair of warps
Ends	Original hems with dark blue silk
Joins	Blue silk stitching through folded butted edges, joining four panels
Colors	6: insect-dyed red, medium blue, light blue, green, ivory, yellow

Transcaucasian (?) warp-substitution-weave silk jajim

Although it is reported that silk *jajim* weaving took place in many parts of the Transcaucasus,[40] silk *jajims* in this format are reputed to be from Sheki and can be quilt top decoration. I have seen thick wool Sheki quilts dyed red, with plainweave silk *jajims*, circa 3' × 5', sewn onto the top. Most of these 'quilt tops' are plainweave, and have insect dyed reds. Warp substitution weave, as here, seems quite uncommon. There are plainweave and complex weave silk horse covers in the trade and in museum collections, as well as a large warp-substitution silk *jajim* that was meant to be a cover.[41]

Many of the motifs in this *jajim* relate to Caucasian pile weaving, if only in a simplified form. The use of two-headed animal forms, as here, is uncommon in these silk warp substitution textiles. The style of using a random order for small devices seems to be similar to that in the pattern in Plate 22.

Silk warp-faced panels from the area may have been produced as 'yard goods' and had multiple uses. Small plainweave double bags made up of the same material are fairly common, with closure areas often reinforced with bits of Iranian silk brocades.

It is conservative to suppose that insect-dyed 'cochineal' silk in these *jajims* is a result of the use of the imported product, either Mexican, or latterly from the Canary Islands, which might lead one to assume late dating. However, there are early silk insect-dyed embroideries which seem to predate local use of the New World dye.[42] The latest analytical techniques can now differentiate between the various red insect dyes, but the effort to determine the source does not seem justifiable in this case.

Transca

ucasus

Sheep and goats belonging to Azeri villagers in the Karachov region, southeast Georgia, early 21st century. Courtesy Rewoven, photo Ryan Carter.

Transcaucasian pile rugs, *sumaks* and *kilims* were produced in such quantity that they can be reasonable to buy and can therefore provide entry points to collecting and learning about Eurasian rugs and textiles. Western private and museum collections have them in spades. But the longer one collects and studies them, the more difficult it seems to become.

With Transcaucasian weavings, it is easy to fall into the trap that equates age with high art value, but it is also easy to think that worn rugs are precious and old. It is hard, on the other hand – once one recognizes that, for a variety of reasons, older pieces are generally more interesting – to collect old rugs, bags and flat weaves in good condition,[43] and not sun blasted, that are perceived by some quorum to be beautiful.

The trick, especially with these rugs, is finding examples that were woven within that aforementioned matrix of peak color sense, conservative drawing that is still innovative, plus sparkle. Trying to acquire examples with these characteristics without buying clever reproductions or substantial rebuilds is often a challenge. Trusted provenance can help mitigate this risk.

They may not be more than nineteenth century village rugs, with production ultimately stimulated by Western commercial demand, but Transcaucasian pile-woven rugs reflect a very diverse group of old design sources, as well as superb dye quality, at least earlier in the nineteenth century. A major reason for the existence of a large design vocabulary is that the Transcaucasus has been situated in a vice between the Ottoman, Russian and Safavid empires, and has served as a passthrough for culture-bearing invaders. This has helped produce a steady population churn. All three neighboring empires have been occupiers of the Caucasus at one time or another and have imposed their design traditions. Trade and migration have also been factors. The variety is remarkable, especially in pile woven rugs, relative to the number of weavers involved – it is said that the whole of the Caucasus in 1800 had only 250,000 inhabitants.

As a result of these factors, there were sources as varied as silk textiles, Indian subcontinent painted and resist dyed fabrics, Kashmiri shawls,[44] Ottoman and Indo-Persian rugs and textiles, Turkic nomad felts and reed screens, and indigenous ceramic motifs for Transcaucasian rug patterns. While it is correct that many pile rug motifs come from a variety of non-textile sources – including glass, architectural, metalwork, miniatures, stucco and ceramics, among others – they seem largely to be filtered through some textile medium.

Indian textile influence is pervasive: a widely used Caspian littoral border design, most commonly found in Shirvan prayer rugs with what look like birds facing left or right within a meander, is a corruption of a Kashmiri design, which in its original form is floral.[45] The *boteh* has the same Indian subcontinent origin, as probably does the use of colonnades for prayer rug '*mihrabs*', taken from *qanats*.

Rugs woven at the design intersection of court and village sensibility have a special appeal. The pile-less weaves mostly come from an earlier tradition, often quite ascetic, and should be considered from a different viewpoint.

Despite what some sophists say, there really is a pretty strong correlation between age and beauty in all Transcaucasian weavings. At the base, the effect of commercial pressure on this relatively small weaving area reduced dye quality, color sense and complexity of design over about a 100-year period, up to almost 1920. Thereafter, for the most part, it was '5-year plan' rugs, quite a different animal. It happened faster in the Transcaucasus than in many other weaving areas in Iran and Anatolia. Synthetic dyes were introduced – a breakpoint is about 1865 – seemingly more quickly than elsewhere, but the real issue with dyes was the reduction of the number of different 'non-synthetic' color combinations used. A good age marker is the color purple, or if you like, aubergine. On the basis of dated examples with believable in-woven dates, the purple used can be a lavender shade that is not much in evidence past about 1865. Indeed, it seems from a study of dated examples, that a peak quality/volume point in Transcaucasian village rug weaving was also reached in about 1865.

Harald Böhmer, assisted by Josephine Powell, was instrumental in reintroducing the aubergine color to dyers in Turkey when the DOBAG project got underway in the 1980s, indicative of the fact that there had been a drop off in purple use in both Anatolia and the Transcaucasus. It is said that this particular early aubergine was time consuming to produce, which would account for its being dropped as a result of commercial pressure. Rather than a variable purple to a dusty lavender (see, for example, plates 32, 34), the aubergine shade used post circa 1865 can sometimes be brownish, even beige, if not replaced by fugitive synthetic dyes.

In relatively early Transcaucasian weavings, that is, from before about 1865, it is fairly common to find three madder shades, including some shade of aubergine, and a large variety of saturated blues and greens, and sometimes two yellows.

Clear, intensely colored wool in these rugs and flatweaves almost certainly reflects sophisticated dyeing techniques. Other than aubergine, a notable early color in these pile rugs is a strong yellow, often used in limited amounts, notably in Plates

Village weaver in Elizavetopol province. Photograph by A. Piralov, 1904. Courtesy Russian Ethnographic Museum, St Petersburg.

40 and 41 (Qarabagh) and as a field color in Plates 35 (Kazak) and Plate 54 (Shirvan). It was apparently produced from a flavonoid source, using a special metallic additive. Madder red dye usage also evolved over the course of the nineteenth century, often from a clear complex red to a nasty brownish color, probably from too much haste in the dyeing process and reduced amounts of dyestuff used. Madder was the basis for many shades and can be controlled by both additives and the temperature of the dye bath. For example, the somewhat unusual dark red/maroon in plates 49 and 54 may be a product of ginger-colored wool placed in a madder bath brought to a boiling point.[46] It is not at all common in most late rugs and may have dropped out of usage because it was too dark. A blue red insect-derived dye (cochineal or kermes), was used in some late pile rug weaving, mostly in the environs of Shusha, in Qarabagh. When combined with areas of madder red, it produces a discordant effect, at least for me.

Undyed beige wool, so commonly used in East Azarbayjani rug weaving, is almost totally absent, except in some relatively early Caucasian rugs; it is a puzzle, because natural beige wool was surely available. Beige tones in most of these rugs are probably a result of the use of a weak madder dye bath.

Was village dyeing institutionalized before 1865? Maybe not, because of the varieties of shades of color used.

A major reason for my interest, especially in pile rugs from the Transcaucasus, is the aforementioned large number of designs used over a relatively short period and the high quality of the dyes used in relatively early pieces. The quantity of designs begs the specific questions about origin and how they developed and changed over time. It appears that sometimes designs moved with the migrants and sometimes remained woven in their original geographic location. Many designs are, of course, derived from early Turkish rugs, but the further east the Transcaucasian production, the more likely the designs come from an Iranian milieu.

All this sometimes makes attribution and figuring out time of production problematic. Some village names used to identify types of rugs are probably accurate, but there is really no way to verify them, based on period studies. However, in the dim, perhaps mythical, past, an Armenian dealer in Belgium allegedly came up with the village names, subsequently popularized by Ulrich Schürmann, that are now most commonly used to identify these rugs in the West. They could be accurate, since Armenians were major traders in the Caucasus and probably would have had access to this kind of data.

Population movements, commercial dissemination of designs, and substantially altered versions of old designs over time add to the attribution problem.[47] I use some village names and disregard others, based on experience, and which of those names are a generally accepted shorthand used to describe a type. Sometimes, I realize, a village name also applies to several nearby villages. I often just use regional names, based on the old local khanate appellation.

These various factors all make this kind of study interesting, but there is more to the story.

There are no documented early Transcaucasian mosque collections of rugs and *kilims* such as have been ferreted out in Turkey by the likes of Charles Grant Ellis and Walter Denny in Divriği, no fieldwork as has been done by the likes of Harald Böhmer and Josephine Powell. No documented idea of what the Transcaucasian villagers or inhabitants of larger towns wove in the seventeenth and eighteenth centuries, other than, presumably, large 'dragon' and 'blossom' carpets. Could the dearth be explained by the idea that '...most of the early ones [were] Turcoman type village rugs, genuine pile weaves for semi-settled former nomadic people?', a product of a small population and a limited commercial market.[48]

Further, since almost all Transcaucasian village rugs date pretty securely to the nineteenth century, it may be that early examples were seized by invaders, but if so, they would surely show up somewhere. Not in the Russian or Transcaucasian museums. But the nineteenth century Transcaucasian dye and weaving quality, the color sense, the variety of patterns surely point to a longer history of some type.

So much material, so little known. The relative lack of data on older Caucasian rugs, the very lack of period fieldwork, leads to easy speculation on origins, sort of a last refuge for art history scoundrels.

Shirin Melikova in Baku reaffirms an old story that the Bolsheviks seized old and new Transcaucasian rugs and sold them in London and says further that there are no records in Azerbaijan that would provide detailed export volume data. It could be the Russians have this data somewhere.

No matter what, there are a lot of imponderables with regard to Transcaucasian weaving. Taking into account early nineteenth century dated examples, there was some early pre-commercial tradition of small rug use, as there was in other rug weaving areas. A few rugs in this collection have in-woven dates that seem to fall into periods before there was much export at all. Perhaps there was more reliance on felt-backed flatweaves, or plain thick felts. It may be that the population was indeed too small and poor to weave rugs similar to those esteemed Turkish mosque collection pieces.

Limited pile rug production, if that was what there was, may have been due to political and economic instability. Melikova says that there is almost no early anthropological information available, that Russification was emphasized, more so in the Soviet period. Elena Tsareva opines that the onset of Russian control, beginning with Georgia in 1802, may have produced the stability and commercial outlets that eventually stimulated Transcaucasian village rug production, and that the Transcaucasus was indeed very poor before the Russian arrival. An annotated folio of watercolor depictions of village life in the Transcaucasus by a Russian artist/ethnographer done in about 1830, would be very interesting, but so far, no luck. Period photographs are not very helpful.

Walter Denny labels Transcaucasian village rug weaving 'commercial', and Michael Franses calls the rugs 'late', both of which are at least partly right. A great deal of rug weaving is commercial and often newer than one wants to believe. But 'commercial', ipso facto, is not evil.

In sum, I am interested in process: How these rugs and flatweaves were made, why they were made, out of what materials, and why the artistic content changed over time. Questions about the age of weavings are answered, sometimes obliquely, in the following narrative; questions about beauty are left up to the viewer.

Kazak

The appellation 'Kazak' for a group of coarse long-piled geometric rugs from the Western Transcaucasus is used in common with a town and district in the Transcaucasus, as well as the Russian 'Cossack', 'Kazakh', a Turkic tribal group from Central Asia, and 'Kozak', a group of geometric rugs from western Turkey. All may derive from Timur's description of himself as an outlaw or brigand.

Because of the variety of structure, Kazak-like rugs that seem older likely came from disparate locations. Some are coarse, long piled, some are fine, long piled and some are intermediate. But by the end of the Caucasian rug boom, Kazak structure was quite standardized.

28

Size	5'8" × 7'2" (173 × 218 cm)
Warp	Z3S beige wool, warps on one level
Weft	Two singles, dark red wool, one to three shots, mostly two
Knotting	V 10, H 8, 80/square inch, 1240/square dm; pile height about 10mm
Selvedges	Two pairs of reinforced warps interlaced with 2 to 5"/5–13 cm segments of wool in all the colors used for pile
Ends	Warp finishes missing; outer 'barber's pole' guard borders missing
Colors	9: red, rose, aubergine, butterscotch yellow, green, medium blue, dark blue, ivory, dark brown, partly corroded

Published: Franses et al., 2017, fig. 10.23

'Lori Pambak' Kazak rug

The field design in this Kazak is dominated by an ancestral Turkmen gul form combined with detached palmettes. The combination seems strange, but the design unit is basically a pendant medallion, and the same theme is applied with different amounts of abstraction in rugs from rural Northern Iran and Anatolia.

In order to fit this Kazak into a context, it is worth considering that pendant medallion designs as here originated with tooled leather Turkish and Persian book covers and were made popular by large Safavid and Ottoman carpets. They appear in village rugs and large workshop carpets all over the Indo-Persian and Turkish weaving areas. Although the field design here, with its distinctly Turkmen-style central medallion/gul flanked by palmettes, does indeed look like an odd and unusual combination, the ivory medallion/gul has design relatives in western Turkish village rugs (*fig.1*),[49] possibly sourced through Turkic migrants moving west in the early nineteenth century, fleeing Russian incursions into the western Transcaucasus.

fig.1 Anatolian medallion rug, before 1800. 5'3" × 6'10" (159 × 208 cm). Metropolitan Museum of Art, New York, Gift of Joseph V. McMullan, 1973, inv. no.1974.149.33.

Elena Tsareva posits that the pairs of green animal-like forms inside the ivory 'gul' are a 'derivation from the Central Asian steppe '*kaikalak*'-type motif... very popular since paleolithic times'.[50] If that is so, they are layered on top of a facsimile of an orthodox Turkmen gul in this rug, which is quartered, has clear crested dark 'birds' on the horizontal axis, and a more stylized pair on the vertical. A presumed local source for this green design may be found in a fabulous late seventeenth (?) century cross-stitch embroidery (*fig.2*), perhaps Armenian, on the basis of the structure, which has the same four pairs of opposed green forms, the whirling dragon center derived from embroideries, and stylized, elaborate crests on the green beasts' heads, and apparent flames, dragon-like, shooting

fig. 1

fig. 2

fig. 1 Transcaucasian silk embroidery, 17th/18th century. 2'4" × 4'3" (71 × 129 cm). Rippon Boswell, Wiesbaden.

fig. 2 Transcaucasian silk embroidery, 17th/18th century. 2'2" × 3'10" (65 × 116 cm). Orient Stars Collection, Stuttgart.

out of their foreheads, but on a red ground (a second similar embroidery exists).[51] The stylized dark brown bird forms with crests on the axes in the Kazak rug are serrated diamonds in the embroidery. Given how similar the medallion motifs are, could the rug and the embroidery be contemporaries? Or is there an intermediate textile that has not been identified?[52] Were the blue and black triangular indents into the red field of the embroidery medallion possibly interpreted by subsequent textile artists – especially Kazak rug weavers – as part of the outline of an archetypal Turkmen gul?

This cross-stitch embroidery in turn seems to be derived from a 'quatrefoil' design (four palmette-like forms radiating at right angles from a center) that probably originated in Safavid court workshops and is used extensively in various versions in later village weaving. A good quatrefoil embroidery example from the Kirchheim Collection is also the basis of a common rug field design, so called 'Kasim Ushag', from the southern Transcaucasus (*fig.3*). Further links between embroideries and Kazaks include not only the field design in the present rug, but others, notably the 'pinwheel' and 'star' rugs. One can therefore surmise that these Kazaks had local embroidery influence, but it is difficult to pinpoint if any specific ethnic group was responsible for the rugs and perhaps also the embroideries, given the movement of peoples throughout the Transcaucasus. The comparison between the rug and the Kirchheim embroidery illustrates once again the fact that there is no sure linear progression from animal forms to more abstraction, and that disparate motifs can be combined.

Other examples of rugs in the same Lori Pambak tradition are illustrated in *Orient Stars*: plate 83 is a simplified highly stylized version with almost exactly the same serrated diamond forms as the embroidery, while plate 82 has the same medallion, with the same interior, but with the medallion in red, as in the embroidery. A more villagey version in the Kaffel Collection, with the same layout, down to a reciprocal outside border, is probably from the western Transcaucasus.[53] It is quite clear how the central medallions in these three rugs devolved from the *Orient Stars* embroidery style. There is also a coarser, more primitive cluster with a similar palmette and medallion design from eastern Anatolia, and a more sophisticated fragment from the same area, half the rug, cut on its vertical axis, is in a California collection. Relatively early examples from both groups are quite limited in number. So, the design had a broad but not deep application across rug weaving areas.

These variant rugs have pendant medallions like those in early Lori Pambak Kazaks, but the central medallions have no animal forms, and the gul shape is not used. Both *Orient Stars* rugs are probably from the same workshop, perhaps in Tabriz. When making comparisons, what is especially interesting is that these similar non-Kazak rugs have, in addition to the pendant medallions very much like those in the Kazak, serrated diamonds on the axes, as in the embroidery.

This Kazak is relatively finely and loosely woven and would not make a durable floor rug. It is possible it was intended as bedding. Old rugs like the present Kazak usually have a grayish purple as a secondary color. Later rugs in this general design are denser and coarser, clearly

made for a market that valued floor-worthiness, probably in the West.

There is another similar Kazak, coarser and with less color,[54] as well as a large fragment that was in the Mitchell and Rosalie Rudnick Collection.[55] A third complete example, whereabouts unknown, has the same border treatment as the Rudnick fragment, and another, in an American collection, is quite similar to the present rug, slightly smaller, with a different medallion center and brindle warps.

It appears this 'Lori Pambak' design suffered loss of its original intent relatively rapidly, especially when compared to the stability of other large Kazak rug designs.[56]

It would be convenient if design development were linear. A possible beginning for the progression in the abstraction of the Lori Pambak design is well illustrated in color by Jean Lefevre;[57] the next stage of design evolution is seen in a commercial period Lori Pambak with palmette-shaped pendants, fused green animals with rudimentary crests in the center medallion and a version of the earlier leaf/meander main border.[58] The final stage is illustrated by a rug in which there is a different border, no crests on the green beasts, and octagonal medallions in place of anything resembling a palmette.[59] These later pieces are often dated, presumably to meet market demand; dates range from the equivalent of about 1895 to 1910. Small Kazaks sometimes have a devolved single Lori Pambak central medallion.

As with many old Transcaucasian rugs, the secondary motifs are of great interest. They virtually disappear in later Lori Pambaks. In this piece, there are three in the field corners, possibly vestiges of spandrels. Generally, the first to go is the ivory 'bug'-like element. In its center is a ram's horn-like form that looks similar to the main ornament in 'Perepedil' rugs. Could there be a relationship?

In one instance, the bug-like ornament appears in a later rug, but simplified.[60] Eberhart Herrmann, in the plate description, could trace his rug's design origin on the basis of having seen pictures of the present Kazak. It is often impossible to figure out the evolution of these Transcaucasian rug designs if earlier versions are not available.

Rugs like this have been called 'Lori Pambak' for years. Lori is a town in Pambak Province in northern Armenia, and the appellation might or might not be accurate, but in any case, it is now firmly attached to this type of Kazak. Present day Armenia, a Persian khanate before the Treaty of Torkmanchai in 1828, concluding a war between the Russians and the Persians, was substantially inhabited by Turkic and Kurdish populations before the Russian conquest. On the basis of census data, Armenians constituted just 21% of the khanate in 1826.[61] So, it is possible that this piece, which, if it is from the Lori area, may date to before the Russian takeover, was woven by Turkic villagers or transhumants, perhaps on a ground loom, as speculated by Lefevre.[62] A seductive idea.

Regarding geographic origin, in 1973 Ralph Yohe, a distinguished collector and an ardent seeker of anthropological information, photographed relatively late Lori Pambak rugs through a window in a mosque in Kars, eastern Turkey. Mosque-donated rugs are often locally woven, so this design may have originated in the Kars region.

29

Size	3'10" × 5'0" (117 × 152 cm)
Warp	Z3S ivory wool, warps on one level
Weft	Two singles, pale red wool, two to four shots, mostly two
Knotting	V 8, H 6.5, 52/square inch, 806/square dm; pile height about 8 mm
Selvedges	Two pairs of reinforced warps interlaced with red wool
Ends	warp finishes missing
Colors	6: ivory (possibly bleached because it is so white) red, medium blue, green, yellow, beige to dark brown

Published: Kaffel, 1998, plate 14

Kazak rug

Kazak prayer rugs themselves do not seem to have a long tradition, but their layout reflects an origin in 'Bellini' rugs. The apparent earliest dated example has a crude date that could be read as 1221 (1806).[63] Since the Shia population of the Caucasus did not commonly use prayer rugs,[64] nor did the Christian Armenians, both of whom were major weavers of these Kazaks, the style was pretty surely driven by external market demand. The design model can be found in a number of Anatolian weaving cultures and may have been brought eastward into the Caucasus as a result of trade and commerce. It may also have been introduced to satisfy market demand for prayer rugs in the West.[65]

The coloration – the chalky white and the deep red – is very close to that of larger Lori Pambak rugs from the second half of the nineteenth century, based on dated examples. For some reason, there are very few prayer rugs like this one.

The structure is like that of most export Kazaks – fairly densely knotted and medium high pile. It is quite different from a presumably earlier 'Lori Pambak' (Plate 28), and no prayer rugs in that weave have come to light. The motifs in this rug are very precisely drawn.

30

Size	5'6" × 6'6" (168 × 198 cm)
Warp	Z2S beige and brown interplied wool, warps on one level
Weft	Two singles, medium blue wool, two to four shots, mostly two
Knotting	V 8, H 8, 64/square inch, 992/square dm; pile height about 12 mm
Selvedges	Two pairs of reinforced warps interlaced with medium blue wool, small amounts of ivory wool, where the blue dye did not take
Ends	Top: ½"/1.5 cm medium blue wool plainweave, following a two-pick obliquely interlaced band Bottom : ⅓"/1 cm medium slightly reduced blue wool plainweave, terminating in original warp loops, some of which are abraded away
Colors	9: red, ivory, dark brown, green, medium blue, dark blue, salmon, yellow, aubergine

Kazak rug

Some older Kazaks, like this example, tend to be less dense, in many cases more finely knotted, have longer pile, more colors, especially (three) red tones, and are precise in their own way, yet less 'mechanical'. The change to shorter pile, denser, coarser knotting and fewer colors was probably a result of commercial pressure, later in the nineteenth century.

This rug is a member of a fairly large cluster of rugs, probably from a village – or several nearby villages – in the Western Transcaucasus, that are remarkably similar in format and layout, as well as in the frequent use of blue wool for wefts and selvedges. It seems the design remained stable in the nineteenth century although some relatively late pieces have different border conventions.[66] Use of synthetic dyes is quite limited, but Ponceau 2R is occasionally seen.[67]

One example in this cluster,[68] is so close to the present rug that they may have been woven by the same women, and another is very similar.[69] The three madder dye colors are the same, as are the guard borders, and the way the ivory brackets are reversed in the horizontal main borders between the *kochanak* forms. Another rug with the reversed brackets and the same guard borders has a clear in-woven date of 1271/1854–55.[70] It might therefore be reasonable to think that this Kazak was woven in that time frame. Many other indicators point to this period as being one in which the output was beginning to grow but the quality remained high. There are other forms of this medallion in Kazaks, as well as elsewhere in the Transcaucasus,[71] but this particular rendition is closest to an Anatolian model.

It is intriguing to contemplate where rug and carpet designs originate, and it is probably a major motivator for collector and academic interest in the field. Regarding the origin of Kazak designs, there are several large-format (ca. 5'6" × 7'0") field designs whose origins can be traced back to much earlier counterparts in Anatolia, and it begs the question of how some but not all came to be woven in the Caucasus.[72] The answer lies partly in common ethnicity, population movements and trade flows.

Walter Denny thinks that these Kazaks '...are (double "outie") symmetrical village renderings of the 'Bellini' (single "innie") design,[73] and thus probably ultimately derive from a gateway representation...', and that they are '...an interesting example of weavers using age-old traditional motifs in a (comparatively) new layout'.[74] This seems a reasonable interpretation by someone who has had long experience in the field.

Denny posits that this evolved Caucasian 'gateway' motif has its seventeenth/eighteenth century predecessors in, for example, four of the rugs in the Turkish and Islamic Arts Museum (TIEM) in Istanbul that were gathered from the great Mosque in Divriği by Walter and Charlie Ellis in the early 1970s. He thinks that the rugs were woven in east and central Anatolia, an area with a large Armenian population at one time, and that some of the larger rugs from Divriği may have come from Armenian churches.

Are these particular 'gateway' Anatolian rugs of Armenian origin? Hard to say. The TIEM rugs are all a bit different, one from the other, more complex than the Kazak version, but they tend to have red fields, the medallion form in red and green, yellow guard borders, and the main border with a dark brown background, very much like the pictured Kazak example.[75] The Anatolian rugs all have triangular spandrels within the square green central portion of the medallion, as well as in the red field, where they bracket the bulbous ends of the central medallion. Some Kazaks in this cluster have spandrels, but

out of proportion with the field, or vestigial spandrels, in the medallion in the form of stars and hooked diamonds.

It was at one time suggested by Joseph McMullan that the blue green color of the central medallion represents a garden or watercourses, which was an innovative idea at the time (1965) but seems a far reach at this point.

It is a puzzle why the more varied and complex Anatolian versions of this design did not make it into the Caucasus, assuming that as a result of trade, the design movement went west to east. There is apparently no early Caucasian version of this design that could be cited as a local source. There is no simple resolution to these issues.

The simplified, stripped down Kazak version of this design, on the basis of dated examples, does not appear to predate the nineteenth century.

This rug is in unworn condition, which is unusual. The background of part of the upper main border may be undyed dark brown wool, as it is uncorroded. It is quite evenly knotted, which seems to be characteristic of this group, but an anomaly for Kazaks in general. The implications are unclear.

These rugs are generally known under the rubric 'Sevan' for a large lake in northern Armenia, and it may indicate where they were woven. But there is no hard evidence to legitimize the name.

31

Size	5'6" × 6'10" (173 × 208 cm)
Warp	Z3S ivory wool, warps on one level
Weft	Two singles, red, blue, rose and beige wool, two to eight shots, mostly two; several red cables to correct curvature
Knotting	V 7, H 7, 49/square inch, 760/square dm; pile height about 19mm
Selvedges	Three pairs of reinforced warps interlaced with red wool
Ends	End finishes missing, but 1"/2 cm of red plainweave remains at the bottom end
Colors	6: red, green, medium blue, yellow, ivory, dark brown, partly corroded

Borjalu (?) Kazak rug

Judging from dealers' lore, and not much else, because there is not much else to go on, this Kazak may have been woven in the Borjalu/Borchalu/Borchali region (or valley) in southeastern Georgia, which is said still to have a substantial Azeri population. On certain maps of Armenia,[76] there is a Borchalu river and presumably, a valley. It is characteristic of this group of rugs to have a main border comprised of offset hooked half medallions, possibly derived from a pattern used in warp-faced pack-bands or *jajims*, and long ago transferred to pile weaving.

There are in this piece characteristics typical of a relatively old Kazak: The high quality of the dyes and the evenness of application; the color intensity and balance; the fact that the structure and the pattern are irregular;[77] and especially quirky elements, like the inner and outer top and bottom guard borders varying in color and design from one end to the other, and different from the side guards. All this seems to reflect unhurried weaving.

The pile seems unusually long for this type of rug. Given the pile length, such Kazaks may at one time have been used for bedding. This rug is loosely knotted but in very good condition. Later Kazaks like this are often more densely woven, with shorter pile. Some older ones may have been sheared, so it is sometimes hard to tell what the pile length was originally.

In contrast to the well-drawn borders, the field is less disciplined. It appears that the weavers had seen a 'Star' Kazak and tried to reproduce it from memory. The ivory field, the two attempts at red eight-pointed 'stars', the box-like forms in the red stars and the green palmettes emanating from the boxes all point to that design origin. Green stars replace blue ones in the original and there are no diagonal hooked forms. For an easy comparison, see the Star Kazak on the cover of *Kazak*.

32

Size	6'5" × 6'7" (196 × 201 cm)
Warp	Z3S uniform ivory/beige wool
Weft	Two singles, dark red wool, two to eight shots, mostly three to four
Knotting	V 6 – 8.5, H 6 – 7, average, 47/square inch, 735/square dm; pile height about 12 mm
Selvedges	Two pairs of reinforced warps interlaced with 1–6"/3–15 cm sections of multicolored wool
Ends	Warp finishes missing; top barber's-pole border missing, but there are remnants of rose wool plainweave at the bottom end
Colors	8: red, ivory, medium blue, blue green, abrashed beige/gold/butterscotch, dark blue, aubergine (partly corroded), dark brown (corroded)

Published: Tschebull, 1971, plate 23

Borjalu (?) Kazak rug

Compare this piece with Plate 14. They come from the same design school, both have nominal ivory fields, but this one seems further removed from the Turkmen-style model. Overall designs of reciprocal hooked forms as here occur on diverse objects, such as Central Asian reed screens, Lakai embroideries, appliqué work, Uzbek mosaic felts, pile-woven transport bags from Fars in Iran, *kilims*, Turkmen rugs, as well, of course, in *sumak* bags from Azarbayjan and the Transcaucasus.

The basic hooked diamond-shaped medallion probably has its origins in early Oguz tribal art, but it is tempting to think this particular Kazak field design originated in pieced mosaic/appliqué felts or broadcloth appliqué. The visual similarities between this Kazak and these other two media are the curved hooks and the lack of 'background versus foreground'.[78] But despite the prevalence of a felt culture in this part of the world, a long-term search has not turned up any 'smoking gun' lookalike Kazak felts – Shirin Melikova told me that Transcaucasian felts are one-color, not with a mosaic structure. Close, but no cigar, are Nogai mosaic felts from the northern Caucasus.[79] But still, there was a 'Kazak' appliqué felted broadcloth horse cover in the Rudnick Collection,[80] and a fragment of one was in a Berlin dealer's inventory at one time, both of which exhibit patterns found in certain Kazak rugs; and there is a similar red broadcloth appliqué textile that was once in the market. There are surely more. They all hint at a broader decorative appliqué broadcloth/mosaic felt component of the local material culture.

One possible reasonably direct Kazak design source is Transcaucasian *sumak* bedding bag side panels decorated with a repeat hooked diamond design on ivory. They are rare. The style is more commonly found on bedding bag sides woven by a group of Azarbayjani nomads who are thought to have summered in the Bozgush Mountains below Sarab in Iran (*fig 1*). It is interesting that what look like riders suspended above four-legged horned beasts on the *sumak* bag also appear on a Kaitag embroidery from Dagestan.[81] Did the Azarbayjani nomads who wove these hooked diamond *sumak* bags migrate south from the western Transcaucasus ahead of the Russian incursion? And were they originally seasonal neighbors of Kazak village weavers? Anthropologists have found evidence of general southward migration.

These *sumak* bag sides have closely placed multicolored diamond-shaped hooked forms that look remarkably like

fig. 1 Azarbayjani nomad *sumak* bedding-bag side panel (detail). Author's collection.

the ones in this Kazak, down to the layering of motifs and the accompanying minor hooked elements. Although settled people would have had little use for most types of transport bags, especially those woven in the sumak technique, there are other instances in which *sumak* designs used by nomads were borrowed fairly faithfully by settled rug weavers (see Plate 39) – and the other way around – so this particular idea of design transfer is reasonable. It would be nice if there were detailed relevant field data and impressions compiled by a folklorist.

It is curious that the use of the field design in this rug, with the pattern made up entirely of hooked forms, seems to have been heavily used for pile rugs in one general western Transcaucasian location.

The square format gives the impression that the rug may have been used as bedding – similar to Anatolian yatak-like weavings – or was based on that model. Coarse long piled rugs like this one are known to have been sheared for floor use by dealers in the West. Did this have much longer pile, typical of bedding rugs, at one point?

A few other examples have almost the exact same field layout – and format in one case – and have the same type of multicolored selvedge and especially the particular way of drawing the half medallions in the side borders – with the bottom hook curled toward the guard border. The implication is that they were likely woven in the same place at about the same time.[82]

The colors in this rug are strong and there is a good aubergine, which probably gives a rough date of production – before the rug boom really got underway.

There are a few knots tied around a single warp. The ivory and butterscotch pile is corroded, which makes the dark blue stand out.

'Borjalu' is probably a tribal name and is used elsewhere in western Iran.

33

Size	5'3" × 8'0" (160 × 244 cm)
Warp	Z3S ivory wool, warps on one level
Weft	Two singles, beige, rose and maroon wool, two to six shots
Knotting	V 7, H 9, 63/square inch, 977/square dm; pile height about 10 mm
Selvedges	Not original
Ends	Warp finishes missing, but there are remnants of red wool plainweave at both ends
Colors	6: red, ivory, green, medium blue, yellow, dark brown, partly corroded

Kazak rug

This rug is curiously successful, at least partly due to its intense color, despite being way outside of the norm. To date, no rug that looks like it has made an appearance. The weavers have adapted what look like slit-tapestry designs in new ways to fill the field and have used an uncommon combination of border elements. The whole composition reminds one of how important design concepts from other textile media were to pile rug weavers in this part of the world. Pile rug weaving technique makes it possible to utilize almost any design, which is part of its appeal.

Although it looks archaic, this rug probably is not. There were Kazak-like rugs woven with hand-spun wool and natural dyes up into the 1930s. Years ago, there was such a Kazak on the market with a clear in-woven Gregorian date of 1939.

34

Size	2'10" × 4'6" (86 × 137 cm)
Warp	Z2S ivory and beige interplied wool, warps on one level
Weft	Two singles, dark red wool, two to four shots, mostly two
Knotting	V 8, H 8, 64/square inch, 992/square dm; pile height about 5 mm
Selvedges	Missing
Ends	Missing
Colors	10: ivory, red, greenish yellow, medium blue, dark blue, salmon/rose, pale yellow, blue green, aubergine, dark brown

Published: HALI 181, 2014, pp. 44–45

Kazak rug

Old is not always good in a rug and good is not always old. But often it is. This ruin, crudely dated 1223 (1808), has a presence made possible by good spacing and drawing and a greater than usual number of colors. Most Kazaks have only six colors, and the use here of ten, including a good aubergine, may indicate that the date is correct. Better and more numerous dyes in a Caucasian rug imply more care and less rush, which may indicate earlier production.

The field and border patterns here are to be seen in other Kazaks,[83] so it appears the design was stable over a fairly long period. At a guess, this style of Kazak was at one time localized, as were many other Kazak types, and early on, there was not a coherent group of 'Kazak' rugs. The field design may be another 'Bellini' derivative (see Plate 30). To know where such weaving originated would be interesting.

It appears the great majority of Kazaks were woven for the export market. If the date in this piece is correct and it is an early Kazak, it probably indicates there was some local commercial market for such rugs. The weaving of Caucasian village rugs may not have really begun in any quantity until the Russians arrived and boosted local economies.[84]

35

Size	4'7" × 9'5" (140 × 287 cm)
Warp	Z3S pale beige wool, some interplied brown
Weft	Two singles, red wool, two to four shots
Knotting	V 8, H 8, 64/square inch, 992 per dm; pile height about 6mm
Selvedges	Two pairs of warps interlaced with red wool
Ends	Top: ¾"/2 cm red wool plainweave folded over and sewn down; Bottom: warp finish missing
Colors	9: yellow, dark blue, blue green, medium blue, orange red, cinnamon red, dark brown, ivory, pale green

Kazak area (?) rug

Sometimes, failing to localize a weaving is what draws a collector in; trying to solve for the unknown can be irresistible. It is difficult to figure out where this rug was woven because it has few structural characteristics that can serve as indicators. In addition, there are very few examples in this cluster to study, especially those with what look like bells, as here, attached by dark lines to the *botehs*.

It may have been a village-specific design. It has been suggested by Bob Mann that the 'bells' may be derived from Turkmen jewelry, which has the same sort of hanging appendages. There are ethnic Turkmen groups in the Caucasus, so the idea is not that out of the ordinary. There are Lakai Uzbek *uut kaps* with similar appendages, too, so specific in-migration might have brought the design from Central Asia.

Jean Lefevre remarked on the difficulty of 'provenance' with regard to almost identical piece with a yellow field.[85] Another similar rug, with a dark blue field, is in Azerbaijan, and a third with a yellow field and with more stylized 'bells' surrounding the *botehs,* was published by Wright and Wertime, probably mis-assigned to the Talish area.[86] There are a few rugs in this group with unadorned *botehs* on red.[87]

Vügar Dadaşov, of Azerbaijan Rugs in Baku, says that this yellow field piece is 'a north west rug, woven somewhere in the lowland (of) Borchali or perhaps (in) the areas adjacent to Kazak.' The structure, which is vaguely like that of many Kazaks, may support this thought, but as he says, regarding origin '...we must remember that the nineteenth century brought the Russian occupation and large migrations in the region.'[88]

Borders in general are quite conservative and often represent a tradition that predates the field design. In this case, the elaborate style of the two reciprocal guard borders is uncommon in the Transcaucasus and has a long history. A rug that once belonged to Vojtech Blau and is a probable member of this group has the same distinctive blue and dark brown guard border and a similar structure. Blau labelled it a Kazak.[89] The Blau rug and the one under discussion here are more finely knotted and have shorter pile than a standard Borjalu/Borchali Kazak.

It is worth noting the range of colors – and their random use – including the intense yellow and the extremely dark, almost black, tonality of dark blue main border background, which are signs of high-quality dyeing techniques. The orange red in the inner reciprocal border is a particular color used mostly in the southeast Transcaucasus, as is the main border style (see Plate 44) and does not seem to have been used much after about 1880. The reasons for this are unknown, but a supposition would be that a cheaper synthetic orange version became available. Less intense yellows were apparently used post circa 1870. Why? Change in demand by importers for color intensity? High cost of concentrated organic dyeing process? Unknown.

36

Size	3'5" × 1'9" (104 × 53 cm)
Warp	Z3S beige wool
Weft	Two singles, pale red wool, one to three shots
Knotting	V 8, H 7, 56/square inch, 868/square dm; pile height about 3mm
Selvedges	Two pairs of reinforced warps interlaced with pale red and red wool
Ends	Top: ½"/1.5 cm pale red wool plainweave folded forward and sewn down with red wool; Bottom: missing
Colors	6: blue green, ivory, red, yellow, dark brown, blue

'Kazak' 'mafrash' pile side panel

A *mafrash/farmesh* is a rectangular box-shaped transport bag of use for nomads in the Transcaucasus and Iran to move and store bedding during migrations, often on camels. There have been a number of 'Kazak' *mafrash* side-like pieces in the reproduction market over the recent past, and the question almost always is, when a piece like this one in such good condition comes up: Is it real? If it is, and this one appears to be, based on different levels of pile corrosion or lack thereof in the greens, blues and dark browns; discontinuous field color which indicates it was woven by two weavers, and the incidental moth damage.

Was this piece really intended to be used as part of a *mafrash* by nomads or transhumants in the western Transcaucasus? There are apparently no complete Kazak *mafrashes* with pile-woven long sides and ends – or *sumak* or slit-tapestry sides or ends in addition to one pile side – although such 'box bags' exist in other Eurasian nomad weaving cultures. And while the top warp finish is folded over and sewn down as are many *mafrash* sides, there is no plainweave at the bottom of this piece that might imply it was part of a bag. It has been speculated that pieces like this were produced commercially in series on a long loom but there are not enough of them to justify this thought.[90] Turkish and Baluch weavers produced *mafrash* side-shaped pile weavings used as pillows but woven from the short side. It is possible that this little 'rug' was intended as a pillow-face, but there are apparently no intact Kazak pillows in this format. There was a similar piece to this one in the market recently, badly worn and with different field ornamentation, making it clear once more that uniqueness is not a characteristic of Caucasian pile weaving.

Qarabagh

Qarabagh is a large mountainous region with a substantial Armenian population. The weavings attributed here run the gamut from flatwoven nomad *jajims* and transport bags to large urban workshop carpets and often cannot be localized.

37

Size	4'9" × 9'11" (145 × 302 cm)
Warp	Z3S ivory/beige wool
Weft	Two singles, beige, pale red, red wool, two shots
Knotting	V 6, H 7, 42/square inch, 651/square dm; pile height about 6mm
Selvedges	Missing, edges reduced
Ends	Missing, ends reduced
Colors	9: red/rose, ivory, abrashed dark blue, abrashed yellow, green, rose, light blue, undyed beige, dark brown

Qarabagh carpet

There are comparatively few rugs like this, and they have often been misidentified. For example, a very similar piece, with similar colors, was cited as being from Konya.[91] Some examples have relatively soft colors and wonky drawing, like this one, and are scarce, which may imply age. The red tone might be the result of a yogurt additive to the madder dye bath. Some in this cluster are drawn with more discipline and have greater color contrast, and it is tempting to think they were woven later.

Most old village rugs do not have sufficient provenance to tell when they were imported into the West, so as to help determine age, but this piece was brought as an antique from the Austro-Hungarian Empire to the US before 1900. However, this is only hearsay, but in the author's family. The presence of *botehs* probably puts the piece in the nineteenth century.

The layout of three blue medallions in the field is fairly common in Caucasian rugs, and a whole class of Kazaks has hooked forms, as here, emanating from their sides. The use of three medallions may reflect Buddhist tradition, according to Charlie Ellis. The motifs in the medallion centers and repeated in the field are found in another type of Caucasian rug, probably also from Qarabagh,[92] so it is fairly certain that this is a Caucasian rug.

This rug has a loose coarse weave and an almost balanced knot structure.

38

Size	2'9" × 4'3" (84 × 130 cm)
Warp	Z2S beige brown wool
Weft	Two singles, undyed cotton, two shots
Knotting	V 8, H 10, 80/square inch, 1240/square dm; pile height about 6mm
Selvedges	Two pairs of reinforced warps interlaced with 1"–28"/3–71 cm. sections of green, red, brown red, and medium blue wool
Ends	Top: 3"/8 cm surviving oblique interlacing Bottom: not original;
Colors	8: red, dark blue, green, ivory, light blue, aubergine/maroon, dark brown, yellow beige

Published: Kaffel, 1998, plate 87

Qarabagh prayer rug

The comparison with Plate 25 (and Plate 26, but without supplementary warp decoration) is too close – the same alternating wide figured red and blue stripes, the narrow guard borders, even the color tones – for there not to have been an almost direct crossover from nomad style to village weaving. One can speculate endlessly on how this happened: Interaction in winter markets, villagers visiting nomads to make felts, intermarriage, and so on.

There is a wide variety of Caucasian pile rugs within which this warp-substitution design concept was borrowed, but largely without the original flatweave motifs. Instead, many of these vertically striped Caucasian rugs feature *botehs* within a meander of some type, as here. It seems a stretch to think that Indian *jamawar* fabric design was a direct source for these patterns just because they contain *botehs*. However, it is true that the *boteh* motif most likely originated on the Indian subcontinent and was in widespread use for pile rugs in the Transcaucasus in the nineteenth century. And there are rugs with lookalike red and white diagonally striped patterns that could be seen as aping Kashmir textiles.[93]

The concept of a *mihrab* intruded into a *jajim* format seems a brilliant innovative idea,[94] but very little in this art form is original, and the same approach can be seen elsewhere.[95] This rug exhibits a rather more successful adaptation of the striped *jajim* look to a prayer rug format because the pattern more or less carries on through the *mihrab* instead of being cut off, as is more common with field designs in many east Caucasian prayer rugs.

The weaver produced a repeat pattern with an almost infinite variety of color combinations and small motifs, which enlivens what otherwise could have been a fairly mundane design.

That this prayer rug is woven with madder rather than cochineal may indicate it may be from before bright 'New World' cochineal use became more common in rural Qarabagh late in the nineteenth century. Further to fixing a date of production, there is evidence with dated rugs from this area as to when they began to be woven with a fugitive purple fuchsin-like dye – about the late 1860s. A good published marker rug, with fuchsin and a clear in-woven 1286 (1870), was in the Harold Keshishian Collection.[96] It is possible that the rug illustrated here predates the common use of both alien and synthetic dyes.

39

Size	2'1" × 7'3" (64 × 221 cm)
Warp	Z3S two ivory, one brown wool, interplied
Weft	Two singles, red wool, two shots
Knotting	V 8, H 6, 48/square inch, 744/square dm; pile height about 4mm
Selvedges	Missing
Ends	Missing
Colors	10: ivory, dark blue, red, dark green, dark yellow, pale yellow, aubergine maroon, dark brown, medium blue, salmon rose

fig. 1 Qarabagh sumak bedding bag side panel (detail), 19th century. Author's collection.

Qarabagh (?) rug fragment

This battered fragment has the motifs and the color relationships of a well-known (probably) Geyiklu Transcaucasian nomad *sumak* bedding bag pattern. Richard Tapper said in conversation that he saw this compelling design on a *sumak mafrash* in 1966, when he was doing fieldwork in East Azarbayjan, and asked about its origin. The owner said her ancestors had come from Qarabagh, bringing the design with them.

At some point, probably relatively early on, judging from the dye quality in the fragment, a village weaver likely borrowed the 'marching peacocks' *sumak* design for use on a pile woven rug (unless one still insists that rugs like this were nomad work) and then adapted it to a long narrow village rug format, transferring a horizontal design to the vertical (*fig.1*). The *sumak* bag side and the fragment are quite comparable when viewed this way. The bird forms in the fragment are a bit more abstract, illustrating how designs can change as they are used in different media and at different times.[97] But it is clear that the weavers knew that they were rendering images of fabulous beasts in the border, because one on the horizontal has an eye and an open mouth.[98]

Where did the nomad and alleged villager exchange design ideas? It might have been at a village dyer, because it seems unlikely that nomads could achieve the midnight blue, among other colors, in the bag side, since it would have required a very time-consuming dyeing process, time that they did not have. Better to acquire the dyed wool in exchange for the undyed product.

A similar fragment, but from a different rug, is in a West Coast collection, and contains a partial Armenian inscription. There is one complete 'marching peacocks' rug extant, but with a runny red, that was on the Web several years ago, and an older one was sold by Rippon Boswell.

Why are there so few of these and why are some badly fragmented? It would seem a popular pattern to weave in pile. Based on the ca. 4' × 8' format of the complete rugs, this fragment is likely about half the original width.

This combination of information sources causes one to imagine that this *sumak* pattern may have been adapted to pile weaving by Armenian villagers, likely in the highlands of Qarabagh.

The use of two yellows here is like that in Plate 34, but it is slippery logic to assume that the rug's in-woven 1223/1808 date is totally accurate and that the similar twin yellows here imply such an early date.

fig. 1

40

Size	3'9" × 10'8" (114 × 325 cm)
Warp	Z3S two ivory, one dark brown wool, interplied
Weft	Two singles, red wool, two – eight shots; one 6"/15 cm long heavy red wool cable on the right side
Knotting	V 6, H 7, 42/square inch, 651/square dm; pile height about 10mm
Selvedges	Two pairs of reinforced warps interlaced with 2"–17"/5–43 cm sections of red, yellow and green wool, inserted irregularly into the body of the rug by up to 3"/8 cm
Ends	Top: red wool weft-faced plainweave folded over and sewn down with red wool Bottom: 1"/3 cm red wool weft-faced plainweave; original warp loops
Colors	7: red, ivory, medium blue, green, yellow, dark blue, black

Qarabagh ('Bahmanli') long rug

Irregular in shape, long piled, coarsely woven, and with strong, clear and even colors, especially a clear bright yellow, this rug is a bit of an outlier among 'Bahmanli' long rugs and would often be called a Kazak. Indeed, it has warp finishes like those of a Kazak.

Böyük Bahmanli, a village on the Aras River in the Fuzuli district of Qarabagh, has been named by personnel in the Carpet Museum in Baku and rug manufacturers in Azerbaijan as the source of a whole group of rugs, with one identifier being the border arrangement seen in this piece. The village name, according to Vügar Dadaşov, is that of a local tribe, which was part of a larger Turkic group that may have settled in the area as early as the Mongol period.

Most of the rugs are shorter piled and a bit narrower than this one, often with an 'egg-palmette' field design, and many were woven with a strong cochineal dye, which was commonly used in the Qarabaghi city of Shusha. Bahmanli is probably best used as regional term, and likely includes the neighboring districts of Jebrail and Fuzuli. No nineteenth century fieldwork confirms the designation.

It has been pointed it out by several scholars, including, possibly originally, Josephine Powell, that the stepped hooked medallion commonly called the 'Memling-gul' may have originated as decoration on reed screens.

The tilt of the fourth 'Memling-gul' field ornament from the bottom was partially corrected by extra wefts and a heavy red cable that is partially visible on the surface of the rug.

Idiosyncratic drawing of the field ornaments offsets the conventional borders, and there is little repetition of color use. The stepped elements in the main border are probably derived from pile-less weaves of various sorts.

Long piled long format rugs like this almost surely would have been used to sit on in narrow village rooms but were woven in the same format for export. This one is too wide for a conventional Western hallway. It is worth contemplating why the Russians did not substantially influence a change in rug formats for export, going for more room-sized production. One issue was the interest in preserving local traditions.

The outside borders in this and the next example are made up of squares of color alternating with elements made up of four 'dots'. It may be that this arrangement of dots mimics structurally driven coarse patterns seen in bast basket weaving. It appears in a slightly different form on the ends of various Iranian nomad *gilims* – usually as five dots – and can be found floating free in rug fields as well as on so-called 'egg' baskets woven by Iranian – and presumably Caucasian – nomads with wool patterning on a rush foundation. The motif surely has a long history.

41

Size	3'4" × 9'5" (102 × 287 cm)
Warp	Z2S beige brown wool
Weft	Two singles, red wool, two shots
Knotting	V 10, H 9, 90/square inch, 1395/square dm; pile height about 6mm
Selvedges	Two pairs of reinforced warps interlaced with red wool
Ends	Top: six rows red wool plain 2/1 *sumak*, followed by a two-pick obliquely interlaced band, some warp ends knotted Bottom: 1"/3 cm beige wool plainweave, with a flat red and green wool braided band with a diamond pattern, sewn on top with red wool, the warps terminating in a two-pick obliquely interlaced band, some warp ends knotted
Colors	10: red, ivory, dark blue, medium blue, green, yellow, salmon, pale blue red, dark brown (slightly corroded), aubergine

Qarabagh ('Bahmanli') long rug

A 'Bahmanli' piece with the same color clarity but with more variety than Plate 40 and more than twice the knot count. Was knot density driven by market price, or was this rug finely woven because that's what the weavers did? Does the large number of dyes used indicate age? There's no way to know for sure, but these factors, plus the finely worked warp finishes, including the braided red and green (the same colors as in the rug) band sewn on over the lower finish, may point to greater care taken by the weavers at a time before significant commercial pressure developed. Only very gentle use would preserve finger-woven/braided bands like this. Such bands are very rare on pile rugs. They are sometimes used on the edges of *jajims* (see Plate 21).

Among the red dyes is a probable insect-based dye that is grayer and paler than the normal 'Shusha' cochineal (which is not a subtle dye in almost all Qarabaghi rugs) and may have been derived from the local 'Ararat' source. Harald Böhmer notes that Ararat kermes produces a weak dye color.[99] An unpublished paper given at a Baku rug and textile conference at the Carpet Museum in 2003 described the culture of Ararat kermes in Nakhchivan.

The medallion forms in the field look like they may be derived from seventeenth century 'Holbein' rugs, but are quite abstract; however, intermediate 'Holbein' forms exist in Turkish village rugs, so the origin is apparent.[100] The Caucasian version of 'Holbein' was used only in the western Transcaucasus, as were many other Turkish designs. This design flow likely illustrates trade movements and Ottoman occupation.

Siawosch Azadi illustrates a similar piece dated 1884, attributed to Jebrail, an adjoining area, with a different border convention, and with apparent less intense coloration.[101]

42

Size	4'3" × 9'6" (130 × 290 cm)
Warp	Z2S beige, brown and dark brown wool
Weft	Two singles, mostly undyed cotton, some beige to brown wool, 2 shots
Knotting	V 8, H 8, 64/square inch, 992/square dm; pile height about 6mm
Selvedges	Two pairs of reinforced warps interlaced with wool in all the colors used in the pile, mostly in 1"/3 cm. sections, but one 18"/46 cm. stretch in green; selvedge wool was inserted irregularly into the body of the rug up to 2"/5 cm
Ends	Top: ¼"/1 cm undyed cotton plainweave Bottom: ¼"/1 cm red wool plainweave
Colors	8: Dark blue, red, ivory, yellow, blue green, aubergine, black, medium blue

Qarabagh ('Bahmanli') long rug

An interesting aspect of the field pattern seen on this rug, which has the clear in-woven date 1253 (1837), is that there is a good pictorial trail that makes the original source relatively easy to identify, as well as how it has evolved over time in rug weaving.

The red and ivory vertical forms in the center of the field, each one different, reflect an Indo/Persian tradition of using cypress tree imagery in miniatures, carpets and especially, printed, painted and dyed textiles going back to at least the fifteenth century. The trees here are radically stylized to such a degree that one only understands what they represent by examining the antecedent forms. The ivory and green apparent clasping curved leaf forms in the field perhaps originated in Ottoman silk and metal thread fabric.

The Azerbaijan Carpet Museum in Baku has labeled a relatively late rug in their collection with this pattern as being from Bahmanli, on the Aras river, and the name might as well be used here, in the absence of any better information. Tantalizing as the name is, the museum can only confirm that long ago Latif Kerimov (born 1908), '...connected [it] with the village of Böyük Bahmanli, Fuzuli district, in Karabakh.'[102] Once again, the lack of 19th century fieldwork limits knowledge.

A relatively early Transcaucasian example with this design, a fragmented carpet in the TIEM, Istanbul,[103] has the same color arrangement – a yellow border and dark blue field as in the pictured rug. The trees are less stylized and there are three horizontal rows of them. The large size of the Yetkin carpet and the ornate design implies controlled weaving; perhaps it was also produced in the Bahmanli area.

In Caucasian rugs of this type, with one column of ornaments, there is an analogue that is so close in design, format and color that it must have been woven at the same time, in the same place, perhaps in a workshop, or some sort of semi-controlled environment, because of the very size, precision, even color, and design complexity.[104]

A somewhat later group of these rugs can probably be dated to the second half of the nineteenth century, based on their relative lack of precision and coarseness of knotting, which allows fewer design elements in the same format, all on a wool foundation.[105] A clearly dated (1289/1872) rug of this type serves as a reference point.[106] These 'cypress tree' rugs are probably all from the same area, because of commonality in ornamentation and borders.

There is a red field example, coarse and on wool, that was at one time in Peter Pap's inventory, and yet another red one with an ivory border and three design elements. A still later group of squarish cypress tree rugs was likely woven in Nagorno Qarabagh, based on color and format.

There are other rugs with similar structure – dense, fairly finely knotted, with mostly cotton wefts, and a large format – that seem to form a cluster, including a Kazak-like design with triple hooked diamonds on red, some 'tree' Kazaks, such as an example in the Metropolitan Museum,[107] and a very similar squarish rug at one time in a West Coast collection, both with a distinctive undecorated medium blue main border, and an octagonal/'Mamluk star' multiple-medallion pattern on ivory. The variety of designs in this cluster of large, structurally similar rugs speaks to how designs traveled around in the Transcaucasus in the nineteenth century.

There is, within the Mamluk Star grouping, a large, striking, ivory-field Kazak-like rug with lots of repair and large eight-pointed stars, and with what I think are cotton wefts, which was stolen from the Dr John Douglass Collection in 2004,[108] and also a closely related, longer-

format, cotton-wefted rug formerly in the Lehmann-Bärenklau Collection.[109] Another related large ivory-ground 'Kazak' rug, also cotton-wefted, is in The Textile Museum in Washington.[110] Eberhart Herrmann illustrates a glorious modified version of the cypress tree pattern on red, probably also from Qarabagh, but with the main curving/clasping design elements described as confronting dragons.[111] The format, layout, and the number of elements pretty much confirm the relationship to the dark blue cypress tree rugs. Borders and field color do not hew to the norm, well illustrating how rug designs could be reinterpreted in the Caucasus, and how plant forms could easily be seen as animals, by both the weaver and the buyer.

The question remains under what conditions these Caucasian rugs were produced. It is romantic to think they were produced by nomads and villagers for love, not money. There are enough rugs with this structure, duplicated patterns, intense color and fairly large format to make me think they come from the same workshop or some type of controlled production, probably early on, based on the inwoven 1253 date in the pictured cypress tree rug. With such an impressive output, one would think there could be some record of this possible workshop. Clearly, years later, with Kustar in control, there were more workshops and established designs, but there is little evidence of this early on. The hunt goes on, but these apparently early rugs might have been woven in Bahmanli.

۱۲۵۳

43

Size	6'0" × 7'8" 183 × 234 cm)
Warp	Z2S wool, red, green, blue, 24 per inch, 61 per dm
Weft	Wool singles, 40 per inch, 102 per dm in the body of the piece; 24 per inch, 61 per dm in the end stripes, the same colors as the warps, plus yellow
Structure	Weft-predominant plainweave with slit-tapestry used where colors meet
Selvedges	Two pairs of reinforced warps interlaced with green, red, yellow and blue wool
Ends	Oblique interlaced band of warp material, terminating with 8"–9"/20 cm, narrow braided warps with ends knotted to secure them
Colors	6: red, green, blue, yellow, ivory/dark brown twining, four rows at each end

Exhibited: MFA, Boston, 2014–15

Qarabagh flatwoven cover

This large textile is finely woven and fragile and was woven in one piece, probably on a wide upright loom, and therefore likely in a village, because of the size of the loom required. It appears to echo a nomad past. Writing of a similar example in the Vok Collection, Hamid Sadighi Neiriz has remarked that tapestry weaves like this are 'called soffreh in Azerbaijan'.[112] There are not very many of them known,[113] and most may have come out of the Transcaucasus post-Soviet collapse. The piece certainly looks like a *sofreh*, although most *sofreh*s are smaller, and its forebears may well have been.

It is remarkable that a textile like this survives, and even with its warp braids intact. It is loosely woven, that is the wefts are not packed down, and it would not survive for more than an instant on a floor, even if it were never walked on with shoes. It has no food stains, nor do others like it. Note that the striped end borders are more coarsely woven. How such pieces survived in such good condition, given their fragility, is a wonder. The fact that they are very similar in format, color and design – even down to the number of brown and ivory lines of twining – militates toward them having been produced in the same community of weavers. In the Vok Collection piece, the blue and green components have been reversed.

The Transcaucasus was the source of other flatwoven covers somewhat like this one which have multicolored warps.[114] There was in the market in Istanbul at one point a similar but conventional heavy weft-faced *kilim* with red, blue and green warps and a zig-zag pattern.

Plate 26 has the same style of braided warp ends. It seems to be a Transcaucasian treatment of warp finishes and may an identifier. The idea of using different colored warps may have been inspired by *jajims*, which use them because of structural limitations. The multicolored warps in this piece match up almost perfectly with the weft colors, which allows for the fragile weave without color distortion and is a tribute to the skill of the weavers.

With these flatwoven covers or *sofreh* or *shadda*, whatever one wants to call them, there is the sense that they were woven in one of the weaving centers along the Aras River, perhaps Bahmanli or somewhere in the Fuzuli or Jebrail regions next door. Because of their generally pristine condition, it appears they were secreted away as savings or retained capital.

44

Size	3'9" × 9'0" (114 × 274 cm)
Warp	Z3S beige wool
Weft	Two singles, ivory wool, two shots
Knotting	V 8, H 9, 72/square inch, 1116/square dm; pile height about 8mm
Selvedges	Two pairs of reinforced warps interlaced with aubergine, blue and red wool; overcast on top, not original
Ends	Missing
Colors	11: ivory, red, dark blue, medium blue, blue green, dark aubergine/maroon, light aubergine, salmon, yellow, beige (probably undyed), dark brown

Sal'yan long rug

This piece is likely from southern Sal'yan, inland from the Kura river delta, near the Moghan and Talish districts.[115] Sal'yan is said to have been a market town for the Shahsavan at one point. The *botehs* in the field place the rug as very likely not earlier than the nineteenth century.

The rug has the characteristic guard borders from the area; the main border medallions, with their vestigial links to each other, are derived from a more complex border style. The maroon and blue narrow guard patterns are borrowed from warp-substitution *jajims*. As with other Caucasian rugs of a certain age, this one, with its large color range, has repeat border medallions each with a different color combination.

The field motif seems to be a local interpretation of a pendant medallion, which harks back to Ottoman and Safavid times (and an even earlier existence on tooled leather book covers),[116] but there are no spandrels – quarter medallions in the field corners – that would imply a never-ending pattern. This merely reflects the distance between this rug design and the original. A similar rug interpretation of pendant medallions can be found in nineteenth century Kurdish rugs from western Iran. Examples of this Sal'yan pattern are rare.

Without folklore studies more or less contemporary with this and other rugs from apparent pre-boom times, it is difficult to know how/if these rugs were used in a local context. One assumes long narrow rugs were meant to sit on in narrow public rooms, and that the format was never changed for the developing export market. It is almost certain that rugs like this were not woven in quantity until there was an export market for them.

Shirvan

Some of the best Transcaucasian slit-tapestry *kilims* come from the general Shirvan area – and a few patterns are converted to pile rugs. Many other 'Shirvan' rugs take their design inspiration from south Asian textiles. Still others source motifs from diverse nomad and court cultures. All three of these tendencies are illustrated by the seven pile rugs that follow (Plates 45, 46, 50–54). The *kilims*, as typified by the three shown here (Plates 47–49), can have a broad array of intense color and unusual designs.

45

Size	4'0" × 7'1" (122 × 213 cm)
Warp	Z2S brown, interplied brown and ivory wool
Weft	Two singles, ivory wool, two shots
Knotting	V 12, H 9, 108/square inch, 1674/square dm; pile height about 3 mm
Selvedges	A pair of reinforced warps overcast with ivory wool
Ends	Each end: 1"/2.5 cm ivory wool plainweave followed by remnants of offset overhand knots
Colors	8: Dark blue, ivory, red, a clear aubergine abrashed to light brown, medium blue, green, yellow, brown/black (corroded)

Published: Cloudman, 1974, p. 47; Petsopoulos, 1979, plate 291; Denny, 1979, plate 43

Shirvan rug

It is tempting to assume the palmette-like design in the field of this rug descends through a long line, harking back to Ottoman textiles. The rug's immediate antecedent is clearly a class of Shirvan *kilims*, woven in some volume, possibly by nomads and then probably settled people. Field studies of this transition, if they exist, would be of great interest.

The fact that warp material and colors are similar implies that the *kilims* and the rugs with this particular palmette design were woven in the same general area. The *kilim* palmette design is rather static, with two basic palmette variations, which would make it seem to have been a relatively recent development, over the course of the nineteenth century.[117]

This rug faithfully copies one of the *kilim* palmette designs in single row of ornaments, and introduces partial medallions at the field margins, in a manner not usually seen in *kilims*. There are not a lot of these pile rugs, and most seem to be from a pre-synthetic period.[118]

The stepped or toothed effect at the edges of the main border on the long side and also along the margins of the palmettes mimics the effect of the structural limitations of slit-tapestry weave, which makes it difficult to render a clean vertical line. In this rug, as in others like it, the toothed effect is also run across the horizontal border edges, which is not structurally necessary in the *kilims* and never appears. The border, which exhibits admirable use of negative space, is lifted from *kilims* also, and has a long Central Asian history. In his anaylsis of Caucasian *kilims*, Yanni Petsopoulos illustrates many palmette examples, including one with the identical 'Memling-gul' border that appears in the present rug.[119] Was its main border copied from that very *kilim*? Petsopoulos had not seen another palmette *kilim* border like it.

Only the guards and secondary field ornaments are what one sees on a conventional Shirvan pile rug.

Orientation of the rug is given by the varied *botehs*, plants and bird forms in the field, all drawn in the style of pile weaving by someone familiar with *boteh*, as used in prayer rugs from the same weaving area, possibly Maraza/Marasali, west of Baku.

46

Size	5'4" × 4'5" (163 × 135 cm)
Warp	Z2S brown, interplied brown and ivory wool
Weft	Z2S beige wool, two shots
Knotting	V 11, H 9, 99/square inch, 1535/square dm; pile height about 3mm
Selvedges	Two pairs of reinforced warps interlaced with pale beige wool
Ends	Missing
Colors	9: dark blue, red, ivory, aubergine, dark red, green, light blue, dark brown, yellow

Shirvan carpet fragment

There is no shame in owning good nineteenth century Caucasian rug fragments. As with the previous rug, this one has a field design that is derived from a Transcaucasian slit-tapestry *kilim*. It is not an exact copy, but the stepped medallion outline and toothed minor borders give its origin away.[120] The fragment likely represents not quite a third of the complete length and the rug originally had approximately six diamond-shaped layered hooked medallions in addition to the red palmette at the bottom. There are a few similar large pieces and many smaller ones; the ca. 5' × 13' format is unusual for Caucasian rugs, not an easy export item, and may have had a particular function in pre-export village life.

The compelling aspect of this fragment is the large number of animals, birds and geometric motifs in the dark blue field, and the fact that border elements are not repetitious in color. A broad range of dyes makes color repetition less necessary. There are three madder tones, including an excellent aubergine.

The main border design, on ivory, is likely derived from a pile-less structure; it was clearly not easy to weave on the horizontal, but the weavers here executed it flawlessly.

47

Size	5'3" × 9'8" (160 × 295 cm)
Warp	Z2S interplied brown and ivory, wool, 14 per inch, 36 per dm
Weft	Wool singles, 48 per inch, 122 per dm
Structure	Weft-faced tapestry weave with slit-tapestry used where colors meet
Selvedges	Pair of warps wrapped with dark brown wool weft returns
Ends	Knotted meshwork with 3 rows of offset overhand knots
Colors	14: Dark blue, ivory, dark red, rose, salmon, beige, medium blue, green, yellow orange, light blue, dark brown, yellow, brown/black, aubergine

Exhibited: MFA, Boston, 2014–15

Shirvan tapestry weave *kilim*

This type of *kilim* often comes with repeat hooked forms on ivory or dark blue and narrow contrasting borders and most likely is from the same area as the ivory and dark blue field prayer rugs. One has to wonder if dark-blue-field flatweaves with repeat designs and contrasting borders like this one, and similar ivory field pieces, had any influence on the design of pile rugs. It seems they predate pile rug production.

This *kilim* appears to never have been used and was not damaged by insect larvae, a remarkable combination of non-occurrences. However, the black in the outside border and in the border elements had completely rotted away, leaving only warps. To retain the visual integrity of the piece and preserve the structure, the black has been replaced.

The interplied brown/ivory warps and the large number of colors place the origin of the piece somewhere in the 'Shirvan' weaving area, probably from a period before the ready availability of synthetic dyes. However, it is a suspicion that Caucasian *kilims* were not subject to the same commercial pressure as pile rugs, and it seems possible may have been woven with traditional dyes for longer. For example, I have seen *kilims* with a broad range of natural dyes, but with small amounts of post-1880 Ponceau 2R brocading which appeared to be original. Could the brocading have been added later? No way to know, but it seems unlikely, since wool brocading was a Transcaucasian weaving, not embroidery, technique.

The broad color range makes the repeat design lively. The field medallions are not in the more common 'V'-shaped arrangement, there is no color sequence, and medallion color combinations are quite varied. Old style aubergine is used sparingly, only in one border element, usage typical of presumably older pile Transcaucasian rugs, bags and flatweaves.

Many of these Caucasian tapestry-woven *kilims* are in about the same format – about 5' × 10' and were probably used – on the basis of my field experience in rural East Azarbayjan houses – as floor covering and covers for piled up bedding during the day. Caucasian pile rug formats were strikingly different.

In addition to tapestry-woven *kilims*, there are in the Transcaucasus, fairly narrow mixed technique flatweaves that are said to have been covers for bulls or oxen.

48

Size	5'1" × 10'3" (155 × 312 cm)
Warp	Z2S brown, interplied brown and ivory wool, 18 per inch, 46 per dm
Weft	Wool singles, 48 per inch, 122 per dm
Structure	Weft-faced tapestry weave with slit-tapestry used where colors meet; narrow pick and pick band at the top end
Selvedges	Two pairs of warps wrapped with red, yellow beige, medium blue, ivory and dark brown wool weft returns
Ends	Top: probably slightly reduced; warp finishes missing Bottom: remnants of knotted warp finish
Colors	6: red, medium blue, yellow beige, ivory, dark brown, maroon

Exhibited: MFA, Boston, 2014–15

Shirvan tapestry weave *kilim*

The spare design is a brilliant concept, almost op art, with brown diagonal elements not quite duplicating and the horizontal stripes being each a little different. It is a surprise that there are not more *kilims* like this.

Lazy lines halfway across the piece, discontinuous lines of color, and some slit-tapestry structure in the plain stripes in the middle of the piece, indicate two weavers were at work.

There is one small maroon motif in the lower left corner. In contrast to the previous *kilim* (Plate 47), the weavers wanted to work with a limited color palette and were quite successful. So successful that the pattern has been used in contemporary *kilim* weaving in Turkey, but in a heavier structure and a squarer format.

The colors are quite oxidized, especially the yellows, which are very pale, and the browns are less dark than when they were dyed. The lack of brown corrosion is noteworthy.

Some Transcaucasian slit-tapestry *kilims* have borders and some do not, and there is no easy rationale for the difference.

49

Size	7'7" × 10'8" (231 × 325 cm)
Warp	Z2S interplied brown and beige wool, 16 per inch, 40 per dm
Weft	Wool singles, 42 per inch, 107 per dm; brocaded incidental forms
Structure	Weft-faced tapestry weave with slit-tapestry used where colors meet
Selvedges	A pair of warps wrapped in dark blue wool weft returns
Ends	Top: two rows of red twining, followed by 1"/3 cm black plainweave; Bottom, two rows of red twining
Colors	14: dark blue, red, ivory, medium blue, aubergine/brown, green, yellow beige, salmon, light blue, maroon, pale yellow green, black (uncorroded), teal, pale yellow

Published: Petsopoulos, 1979, plate 298

Shirvan tapestry weave *kilim*

Kilims were not heavily sought after in the export market, and it is said that they were often thrown into pile rug shipments for padding. That is possibly how this piece ended up in the West. It is unusually large for a Shirvan, so large that it had to be made up from two separate weavings. The design of stepped diamond forms flows pretty well between the two halves. Did the format have a specific purpose?

The draw here is the large variety of colors, which are very similar to those in Shirvan pile rugs from before the advent of synthetic dye use in the eastern Transcaucasus. One marker color for the period is dark red/maroon, here used in small quantities. The brownish aubergine is typical for a number of older Shirvan area pile rugs as well as warp-substitution *jajims*, as in Plate 23. The variation of color use in the stepped diamonds, made possible by the number of dyes available, and their random order of application, are marks of unhurried weaving, and might be an age indicator. Sometimes these *kilims* have in-woven dates, but not very often.

The border in this piece seems not to relate to any common pile rug border.

50

Size	4'10" × 13'3" (147 × 404 cm)
Warp	Z2S brown, interplied brown, beige and ivory wool
Weft	Z2S undyed cotton, one to two shots
Knotting	V 9, H 8, 72/square inch, 1116/square dm; pile height about 5mm
Selvedges	Two pairs of reinforced warps interlaced with faded pale blue cotton
Ends	Top: oblique interlaced band following ½"/1.5 cm ivory wool plainweave; Bottom: warp finishes missing
Colors	11: light blue, ivory, rose red, salmon, green, yellow, dark blue, dark brown, light blue, aubergine, 'khaki'

'Akstafa' long rug

'Akstafa' is surely a misnomer for this type of rug and it would be interesting to learn how they came to be misnamed. The town of Akstafa is quite a distance west from where this piece was apparently woven. Kerimov and Azadi place production of these in Sal'yan, reasonably close to the trading center of Baku, and a believable location. According to Vügar Dadaşov, it could also be from adjacent south Shirvan, but in any case, the rug type is fairly well localized. The warp composition is a Shirvan indicator.

There are quite a few 'Akstafa' rugs; most have wool warps and somewhat brittle cotton wefts, a large array of relatively soft colors, including three red tones in older pieces – but usually one being an aubergine dye – and a long narrow format. One has to ask why the low contrast colors and why are they so consistent? The beige tone is almost certainly dyed, probably in a weak madder bath with additives.

The most usual field design is eight-pointed medallions alternating with inward-facing birds.[121] There is a tradition of opposed birds in early Anatolian rugs,[122] and there are opposed creatures on each side of a tree-like form dating back to at least early dynasty Egypt, but there is no apparent opposed bird design evolution in Caucasian village rug weaving. It looks like the 'Akstafa' motif, with skeleton trees between the birds, was lifted from various sources, and the birds especially, from the *sumak* bag weaving tradition, and gussied up.

This rug has what look like zoomorphic motifs alternating with generic layered hooked medallions. It is another example of probable transitions from floral and other formal designs to animal-like forms and back, with little in the way of age-related factors.

Large format rugs like this are not very common. Most of these large (ca. 5' × 13'/152 × 396 cm) rugs are in the design seen in a fragment from a similar format rug (see Plate 46). A good folklorist might have been able to record how such rugs were used domestically, if they were.

One of the best features of older large format eastern Transcaucasian pile rugs like this Akstafa and the illustrated fragment is the number and variety of minor ornaments that fill the otherwise empty areas in the field, in this case, in no particular order. In addition, the rug width allows for guard borders that depict animals and humanoids. The discontinuous main border, with three different sets of ornaments at the beginning of the rug, is probably the product of unsupervised weaving.

The impression given by this group of rugs is that they do not have a longer tradition, like, say, Kazaks, and may have developed quickly as a result of relatively late commercial demand, but still early enough to have mostly good dyes. And they are attractive. The opposed bird forms in the field were used in late 19th century Kazak-like weaves, but that use also appears to have no long history.

51

Size	3'4" × 11'2" (102 × 343 cm)
Warp	Z3S brown, ivory/brown interplied wool
Weft	Z2S undyed cotton, two to four shots
Knotting	V 10, H 8, 80/square inch, 1240/square dm; pile height about 6mm
Selvedges	Two pairs of reinforced warps interlaced with oxidized undyed (?) cotton; some replacement in wool
Ends	Remnants of ivory wool weft-faced plainweave
Colors	11: blue green, ivory, red brown, rose, medium to light blue, light brown, yellow to beige, dark aubergine, dark brown/black, beige undyed, maybe camel-hair, orange/beige

Shirvan long rug

Undecorated fields in pile rugs are thought in some quarters to have been derived from *sofreh* – flatweaves on which nomads served food.[123] The triangles indented into the field reinforce this idea, as they are stepped, just as are designs in slit-tapestry weaves.

This rug, probably village weaving from south Shirvan, is a member of a small cluster of survivors, all with the same border convention and stepped indents in the field.[124] The outside reciprocal border, woven with corrosive dark brown and blue, is fragile, and is missing in three other similar rugs.[125]

Two examples with almost identical designs to this rug, down to the way the end borders are drawn, are generally described as being from East Azarbayan, in Northwest Iran.[126] It would be remarkable if the design were transferred so precisely over such a relatively long distance, but population movements could produce such a phenomenon. It is just that they are for the most part not documented.

The main border here is tightly spaced, so that there is a strong feel of the negative space between the elements. There are other iterations of this style of long rug,[127] often with red fields, and with a more open main border design. And there is a rug in the same cluster with an attenuated 'Harshang' design.[128]

The rugs in this group are all in long-rug format, so it seems that similar *dozars* and prayer rugs may not have been woven early on. But the sample is small. It may be that later in the nineteenth century this area was producing rugs with different designs and in different formats. One implication is that these few long rugs are pre-boom weavings.

Typical of rugs like this, there is a sparse use of a clear purple.

52

Size	3'9" × 7'11" (114 × 241 cm)
Warp	Z2S beige and ivory wool
Weft	Two singles, undyed cotton, 2–4 shots
Knotting	V 8, H 8, 64/square inch, 992/square dm; pile height about 4mm
Selvedges	Left side, two pairs of reinforced warps interlaced with undyed cotton; right side, one pair of reinforced warps wrapped with undyed cotton
Ends	Warp finishes missing
Colors	10: ivory, rose, medium blue, light green, dark blue, blue green, medium brown, yellow, light blue, dark brown (uncorroded)

Shirvan lattice design rug

As with a number of older Transcaucasian rugs, this piece holds the attention with a repeat design but with constantly changing color combinations. Since the field design, with its sharply defined lattice, probably reflects an abstraction of more explicitly floral antecedents, one can imagine it oriented so that the smaller diamond forms are placed below the larger diamonds – reflecting the original character of the flowers within the lattice from which they derived.

There was a flood of Indian and Kashmiri textiles into Iran and Europe starting in the mid-seventeenth century.[129] This continued into the period of the Russian conquest of the Transcaucasus and the beginning of the production of ivory-field rugs with diagonal or 'V' shaped geometricized floral designs within a contrasting diamond lattice. This lattice design innovation can be seen in Kashmiri textiles from that same period and a bit earlier. Such Indian subcontinent textiles reached Baku in some quantity, and there are examples in the National Carpet Museum, the National History Museum, and the National Museum of Art, as well as in private collections in Azerbaijan.[130]

Alternatively, some Indian-style textiles that reached Baku may have been Persian in origin, but Persian production at that time must have been much less, if only given the size difference in populations between Persia and India.

The ivory field seen in these Caucasian rugs may reflect the use of undyed cotton in Indian *palampores*, which are painted and printed textiles, or the ivory pashmina used in Kashmiri textiles. Most of the ivory field rug production appears to have taken place near urban centers such as Baku and Shamakhi.

In this rug the main border elements have a large variety of different color placement. The background color in the main border is a rose tone seen in other finely knotted 'Shirvan' rugs, notably so-called 'Chajlis'. This rose is a color that seems to have dropped out of use later in the nineteenth century. The quality and number of dyes points to fairly highly developed local weaving/dyeing culture.

Most rugs like this, albeit in a more squarish format, have prayer niches, but there is no Shi'a tradition of using them, so they are surely a creation of commercial demand. A tipoff here as to when they were first woven is that there are no ivory-field prayer rugs dated earlier than 1807, on the basis of Kurt Erdmann's study of rugs with woven-in dates.[131]

There is one very similar piece, published by Eberhart Herrmann,[132] who thinks his rug dates to the first half of the nineteenth century. Absent any documentation, it is easier to call these rugs 'pre-boom' and leave it at that.

53

Size	4'0" × 4'8" (122 × 142 cm)
Warp	Z2S beige, interplied brown, beige and ivory wool
Weft	Two singles, ivory wool, 2–3 shots
Knotting	V 12, H 10.5, 126/square inch, 1953/square dm; pile height about 6mm
Selvedges	Two pairs of reinforced warps interlaced with medium blue wool; abraded and rewrapped in places
Ends	Warp finishes missing, outside guards partially rewoven; probably had knotted warp finishes, based on other examples with complete ends
Colors	9: ivory, red, dark brown (partially corroded), dark blue, pale to medium green, orange yellow, medium blue, aubergine, beige

Published: Kaffel, 1998, plate 47;
Franses et al., 2017, fig. 10.20

'Perepedil' 'prayer' rug

It is of course difficult to know whether woven-in dates are accurate. In the case of this rug, the weavers were emphatic, crudely dating it in six places, correctly and in mirror image, 1281/1863. How does one know if the date is real? One way is to find similar rugs with similar in-woven dates. One in the Museum of Applied Arts, Budapest, is dated 1272,[133] which tends to make one think the 1281 date may be accurate; the rugs have the same field layout, except that those infernal diagonal bird-like forms are not present in the illustrated rug, and because they have the exact same borders. A third Perepedil rug in a California collection has almost exactly the same format and borders as in the present rug, and the bottom left 'ram's horn' field element has the same reversal of its lower volute; however, it is undated. It is possible the same women wove all these rugs. The lack of the bird-like forms and the wider format here allow the design elements to be more spaciously drawn.

The rug has a good clear light-fast aubergine, which may help document when that dye fell out of general use. It seems that it was woven a bit before synthetics first appeared in quantity in Caucasian rugs. Early synthetics featured a strong purple, albeit fugitive, and the madder-based purple was allegedly hard to produce (see Plate 38 for more detail on aubergine dye).

There is a fair number of these 'Perepedil' ivory field prayer rugs extant, some with the same border convention as here, and Ralph Kaffel is probably right when he writes that those with ivory fields tend to be older than those with red or blue fields.[134] Late Perepedils are usually cramped and more highly stylized in design. The best grouping of ivory-field examples is in Ralph Kaffel's *Caucasian Prayer Rugs*.[135] Most have the diagonal bird forms in the field. It seems reasonable to assume that they are stylized palmette forms derived from embroideries, and perhaps the 'ram's horn' forms are too.[136] Other nineteenth century Caucasian village rugs also have designs that are derivatives from a variety of media.

Years ago, there was a ca. 2 × 3.5-meter carpet in the trade with a Perepedil design on yellow, but the design seems primarily used for small rugs. A rug with the basic Perepedil design on ivory in the Burns Collection seems to be from another part of the region.[137] There must be a few others like the Burns piece, which is coarser than so-called Perepedils, and with different border conventions. Dating is problematic.

On the basis of the structural analysis of four ivory field Perepedil rugs published by Kaffel, the present piece is, on average, an astounding 80% more finely knotted.

The main border has Turkish village rug antecedents, and it appears in earlier Caucasian rugs.[138]

54

Size	3'6" × 4'5" (107 × 135 cm)
Warp	Z2S beige, uniform ivory wool
Weft	Two singles, undyed cotton, 2 shots, occasionally 1
Knotting	V 13, H 9, 117/square inch, 1814/square dm; pile height about 3mm
Selvedges	Sightly reduced
Ends	Slightly reduced
Colors	8: yellow, ivory, green, dark blue, red, light blue, abrashed, maroon, dark brown

Shirvan rug

There are a few other rugs like this, and they are all in long format.[139] This example is in a dimension common for prayer rugs, and is probably not unique, but other similar examples with these colors and this ornamentation are not at this point identified. The members of this group of rugs exhibit the same border conventions, down to the guards and the same field color, which may be an imitation of a common color used in silk Caucasian embroideries. It is likely that, because of the complexity of the ornamentation and the limited number of extant examples, these rugs were woven relatively early, which means different things to different people. They are all probably from the same village.

The longer/larger rugs in this cluster are a bit coarser than this squarish example, and often have wool wefts as well as warps. In a presumed effort to produce a finer fabric, the weaver here used (thinner) cotton wefts, which broke in several locations and had to be restored, a fairly common situation with some rugs from the eastern Transcaucasus.

There were many different paths for design evolution with these village rugs. In this case, it looks like a version of mix and match was used, much as with Plate 53, but exactly how it developed will never be known. The blue central medallion is in the configuration of a Turkmen Chodor gul, a form that is fairly common in Sivas area long rugs,[140] and it in turn contains two ivory forms that appear in Transcaucasian/Azarbayjani nomad *sumak* bedding bags. The green cartouche-like elements at each end of the field look very much like they were lifted off an earlier style of Caucasian workshop rug.[141] This cartouche form is likely originally an escape from a large Safavid carpet.

The same field design, but on a red background, appears in some Qarabagh pile rugs, albeit in a cruder version because the knot count is lower.

Quba

There are many different types of rugs listed under the 'Quba' rubric, but a good set of identifiers to use, at least with older pieces, is to look for those with four borders, slightly depressed warps, conservative designs, three-cord mostly blue selvedges, warp finishes terminating with five rows of offset overhand knots, and tone on tone reds. Later examples tend to have a greater variety of patterns and much less luminous and harmonious colors.

55

Size	3'6" × 6'6" (107 × 198 cm)
Warp	Z4S ivory wool, alternate warps slightly depressed
Weft	Two singles, ivory wool, 2 shots
Knotting	V 12, H 9, 108/square inch, 1674 per dm; pile height about 5mm
Selvedges	Three pairs of reinforced warps interlaced with faded blue cotton inserted irregularly into the body of the rug up to 3"/8 cm at bottom end, but ¾"/2 cm otherwise
Ends	Knotted meshwork with 5 rows of offset overhand knots, following or preceding four rows of light blue faded cotton 2/1 *sumak*
Colors	10: dark brown, red, ivory, medium blue, green, yellow, pale rose, dark blue green, dark red, aubergine

Quba 'Lesghi Star' rug

In the relatively small world of Caucasian rug studies, there is hardly a more controversial subject than the origin of the 'Lesghi Star' motif used four times in the field of this rug. Could it have grown out of restrictive *zili* or slit-tapestry structure?[142] Is it an atélier-sourced nineteenth century construct, developed perhaps in Baku or Shamakhi?[143] Is it developed from repeat octagons? Eight-pointed stars? Misinterpretation of background for foreground from an earlier motif? Charlie Ellis thought it may have evolved from Ukrainian textile designs.

Among the more likely explanations, the stepped appearance of the 'Lesghi Star' does mimic Anatolian *zili* structure,[144] or, indeed, slit-tapestry weaves, but there is no trail of design evolution to follow. It seems unlikely that the Lesghi Star is based on a new nineteenth century design – there is no evidence to support this. The eight-pointed star is a stable old design that does not seem to change – there are no stages of morphism into the Lesghi Star.

So, the origin of this motif is not clear. The stepped 'Lesghi Star', is neither strictly Lesghi, a tribal group in the northeast Transcaucasus, nor, most likely, a star. The primary weavers of these rugs in the nineteenth century in the northeastern Transcaucasus were largely local Turkic peoples and Tats, but possibly also other indigenous ethnic groups, maybe even some Lesghis.

Could migration have brought the design into the Transcaucasus? One probable source is Anatolia. There are a number of old Turkish village rugs that have almost Lesghi Star patterns – seemingly derived from 'Holbein' style medallions – that are tantalizingly close to what appears in this Caucasian rug. The apparent oldest of these is in the Vakıflar Museum in Istanbul, a rug with a disjointed meander border, probably from central Anatolia.[145] Another apparent later version, probably from western Turkey, and maybe early nineteenth century, was in The Detroit Institute of Arts. There are other Anatolian village versions. One example, with a 'star' almost identical to that seen in Qubas, but with much different coloration, is published by Brüggemann and Böhmer, who speculate that the star evolved as a result of color change within octagon designs.[146]

It seems plausible that the 'star' went through a process in which it was changed from a quasi - 'Small Pattern Holbein' medallion into a 'Lesghi Star', perhaps with nomads as vectors, who gave it a stepped, straightened form due to structure restrictions, was converted into its present form in a different medium (*sumak?*), and moved east by migration and commerce into the Caucasus where it became a design for settled rug weavers.[147]

There are several Lesghi Star *sumak* versions in various types of transport bags from the Transcaucasus and northern Iran. There are Ukrainian textiles in the Robert Chencener Collection that mimic the Lesghi Star and it is precisely drawn in a double interlock tapestry Swedish cushion cover in the Lloyd Kannenberg Collection. And it also appears on primitive structure 'one warp double cloth' south Persian pack-bands. These bands and their designs may well have a history as bast structures dating to Neolithic times. Such a wide distribution in different media, locations, and formats militates toward a reasonably long history.

So, the broad distribution of the Lesghi Star probably illustrates how important population movements are to design commonality. If the dissemination of the Lesghi Star design could be precisely pinpointed, perhaps a chronology could be constructed. In any case, somehow, these early star-like 'Holbein' designs probably evolved into the 'Lesghi Star'.

The design elements in this rug are precisely drawn, there are border corner solutions, the colors are clear and even, and there are minor motifs in the field that do not appear in most rugs of this type – two kinds of palmettes, ascending plant forms, and little heart-shaped elements pointing inward from the edge of the field. All this points to unhurried weavers.

The rug is wider at the bottom than the top, as the wefts were pulled less tautly at the beginning of the weaving.[148]

The edges and warp finishes are intact, but the dark brown field was, on acquisition, completely corroded away. The decision to replace it was motivated by the fact that the design was lost on an ivory warp and weft foundation. Replacing corroded dark brown fields in old Caucasian village rugs is done on a case by case basis – there is no rule.

There is no hard evidence that the 'Lesghi Star' pattern used in Transcaucasian rug weaving predates the nineteenth century in its present form. Is that because the design had not been introduced into the Transcaucasus earlier? Questions, questions.

56

Size	3'5" × 5'3" (104 × 160 cm)
Warp	Z4S sections of interplied ivory and brown as well as straight beige wool
Weft	Two singles, ivory wool, 2 shots
Knotting	V 12, H 8, 96/square inch, 1364/square dm; pile height about 6mm
Selvedges	Two pairs of reinforced warps interlaced with dark aubergine wool
Ends	Top: remnants of aubergine wool plainweave; Bottom: warp finishes missing
Colors	12: ivory, medium blue, red, light blue, pale green, dark blue green, aubergine, dark yellow, dark red/maroon, pale yellow, beige, corroded dark brown

Quba 'Memling-gul' rug

Contained herein are all the characteristics that can make these weavings so sought after – a precise conservative design, wide and compatible color range and ever-changing color combinations. The trick for a good weaver of these rugs was to work just within that conventional design vocabulary and use seemingly random color combinations to make things interesting.

Named for its appearances in paintings by Hans Memling (1430–1494), the field motifs and layout seen here, of Central Asian ancestry, are ubiquitous in Anatolian and Caucasian pile rugs, and also found in pile-woven bags, reed screens, brocades and embroideries. Transcaucasian embroideries, presumably earlier than this rug and from the same area, are decorated in the same compartmentalized 'Memling-gul' style.

Aside from the unusual color combination used, including two yellows and undyed wool, there are aubergine selvedges and an aubergine partial weft-faced plainweave end finish at one end.

The diagonally striped guard borders are characteristic of period Quba rugs and are almost certainly derived from a larger scale embroidery border. An example is in a fragment that was at one time in the Rudnick Collection. The same guard appears in Plates 53 and 55. It seems likely that the embroidery style was produced in the same area, because this guard border design is pretty much confined to rugs from the northeast Transcaucasus.

It is reasonable to guess that the piece was woven before the late 1860s, when synthetics started to come in, but it is impossible to pinpoint a date. But, assuming 1860 as a date of production, it is quite astonishing to realize that within another generation or so, the quality of these Qubas declined markedly, despite, or maybe because of, the Kustar project set up by the Russians, meant to revitalise rug weaving in the Caucasus. Kustar is yet another illustration of how difficult it is to revive folk art once living conditions and values have changed.

57

Size	2'7" × 3'5" (79 × 104 cm)
Warp	Z4S undyed cotton, alternate warps depressed
Weft	Two singles, ivory wool, 2 shots
Knotting	V 11, H 8, 88/square inch, 1488 per dm; pile height about 5mm
Selvedges	Three pairs of reinforced warps interlaced with green wool, inserted irregularly into the body of the rug up to 3"/8 cm. but mostly 3/4"/2 cm.
Ends	Five rows of green wool 2/1 sumak, followed a two-pick obliquely interlaced band with up to four rows of terminating knots
Colors	9: ivory, dark brown, dark red, dark blue, medium blue, rose, light green abrashed to dark blue green, yellow, aubergine

Quba/Zeikhur rug

This rug has the 'tone on tone' reds of Qubas and Zeikhurs, but is somewhat of an anomaly, given its structure. It is probably from the north end of the Quba weaving area. The lack of color repetition here is the mark of a skilled weaver; there is quite a bit of variability in the green and rose dyes.

As with many Transcaucasian village rug designs, what appears here does not seem to have long antecedents, other than as part of some vague Turkic vocabulary. But these Transcaucasian rugs, the relatively early ones at least, were woven with such skill and with such good wool and dyes that it is hard to imagine that some designs just suddenly appeared, fully developed, as late as the early nineteenth century. But this is a thought worth pondering.

Known in Western rug literature as the *khirdagyd* design, the field pattern here of *botehs*, palmettes, 'comb animals' and rosettes is apparently more correctly named '*khirdagül*', or 'small flower' in Azerbaijani Turkish,[149] and the name may be a carryover from earlier times. It is said to have originated in Chichi villages in the northeast Transcaucasus and could be an example of a design created to meet demand for variety in the nineteenth century. There are quite a few versions; an early one, in which the only element that is common to others of the same cluster is the palmette, is dated 1282/1865.[150]

The structure is quite dense, with alternate warps depressed and knots packed down harder than is usual for a Quba. Cotton warps used here are uncommon in these rugs and probably add to the density. One of the consequences of the structure is that the dark brown portion of the field is intact. A somewhat similar design, has similar selvedges and an apparent dense structure, described by Ian Bennett as 'ribbed'.[151]

There is a tiny amount of aubergine within the 'serrated leaves' in the main border. Limited dark aubergine is fairly common in older Caucasian rugs, and it may indicate the dye was expensive. It is fairly easy to see the ivory negative space as serrated half medallions in the main border.[152]

Because the cotton warp finishes are intact and there's no wear, it is apparent that this rug has done little floor time.

Zeikhur

A series of villages in extreme northeastern Azerbaijan and southern Dagestan were the probable source of marvelous pile rugs that have been marketed under the name 'Zeikhur' or 'Seychour'. The village name, Zeikhur, was transliterated into its present form by Richard Wright, a prominent scholar interested in aspects of Transcaucasian weaving.[153]

Travel in the region would have been slow and difficult in the nineteenth century, allowing isolated communities to develop, and probably accounting for the difference in design and structure between what are now called Zeikhur and Quba rugs. The weavers of Zeikhur rugs, apparently because their production area was closer to the Caspian coast and thus relatively more accessible to metropolitan Russia, were earlier to adopt alien designs such as abstract patterns and European-style roses.

But village weaving or not, there was a definite level of sophistication there, because many Zeikhurs have out-of-the-ordinary field designs that were inspired by silk embroideries, European patterns, tile work, South Asian textiles and large carpet motifs. Pointing to a degree of urbanized production, dragon carpets,[154] and large *sumaks* can be ascribed to the Zeikhur area.

Nineteenth century Zeikhurs commonly have wool foundations, blue wool selvedges and *sumak* end-stopping. Characteristic main borders have a wide blue and ivory 'wave' design, often with an inner border of red tone-on-tone linked star forms. The typical inner border may be derived from workshop rugs.[155] It also appears on some *sumak* bedding bags, often with greater color contrast, perhaps acquired through nomad contact with settled weavers.

58

Size	2'4" × 4'0" (71 × 122 cm)
Warp	Z3S ivory wool, alternate warps slightly depressed
Weft	Two singles, ivory wool, 2 shots
Knotting	V 10, H 9, 90/square inch, 1395 per dm; pile height about 4mm
Selvedges	Three pairs of reinforced warps interlaced with (dyed? the question because the color is so consistent) beige wool
Ends	Knotted meshwork with (probable remnant) 3 rows of offset overhand knots, following or preceded by four rows of light brown (dyed?) wool 2/1 *sumak*
Colors	9: dark brown/black (mostly corroded out), aubergine, red brown, ivory, medium blue, dark aubergine, green, yellow beige, salmon

Zeikhur rug

Palmettes are ubiquitous field designs in Caucasian rugs and flatweaves, in many iterations, and have a long history in Islamic and Asian Art. Sometimes, they fill out the whole field of a rug or carpet or *sumak* with large directional forms.[156] It seems probable that ascending or directional palmettes as a field design are derived from more complex compositions in which palmettes point in several directions.

In the case of this unusual Zeikhur, the design antecedent was possibly a series of large palmette carpets from Kurdistan, thought to date to the eighteenth century, such as an example in the McMullan Collection, also cited in the text to Plate 1,[157] in which the interiors of several palmettes are very similar to the palmettes in this rug; the simplified trident form seen at the top of the palmettes in the Zeikhur is prominent in the large Kurdish carpets. The complete Kurdish palmette form was widely used in Azarbayjani export rugs and carpets in a '*Harshang*' design.

Traditional Zeikhurs have the two borders described above and very limited guards. Since the weaver scaled all the design elements to fit this rug's small format, the main border is one that is normally used as a narrower secondary. And the inside border, rosettes on aubergine, is squeezed for space, so there was no room for the usual attached hooked forms that imply a connection between the rosettes (see the inner border of Plate 60 for comparison).

In the field, there is one humanoid decapitated by the top border, an apparent blue tulip, and seven backwards and forwards swastikas – the latter can be observed as running decoration on the edge of women's clothing in Hellenistic sculpture, for instance on a statue in the Acropolis Museum, on which the design is painted in purple, now mostly gone.

The fact that the brown/black knots in the field have almost completely fallen out of the foundation, even though the rug has hardly spent any serious time on the floor, may be an indication that the rug is older than most. The amount of corrosion in this field is part of the allure and does not detract from the design.

The side and end finishes in this rug are absolutely typical for Zeikhurs, with the exception of the light brown color.

59

Size	4'0" × 8'10" (122 × 269 cm)
Warp	Z3S uniform ivory wool
Weft	Two singles, brown to dark brown wool, two shots
Knotting	V 12, H 8, 96/square inch, 1488 per dm; pile height about 5mm; knots densely packed
Selvedges	Three pairs of reinforced warps interlaced with dark blue wool, inserted irregularly up to 7"/18 cm into the body of the rug
Ends	Three rows of medium blue wool 2/1 *sumak*; knotted warp-finish apparently cut off
Colors	11: Dark blue, red, ivory, dark red, medium blue, rose, light blue, green, yellow, red brown, dark brown

Published: Tschebull, 1992, plate 8

Zeikhur 'Vase' rug

The piece is dated 1277/1860; four places backwards in the lower main border and three times correctly, but upside down in the upper border. So, it is probable that it was not woven before that date. The high quality of the dyes and the lack of synthetics tend to confirm the in-woven date.

Taxonomy is, indeed, king. Armed with a probable date, it is possible to engage in informed speculation about the conditions under which this rug was woven. It is relatively large, dense, has an unusually large number of very evenly dyed colors, and has a very complex, fairly precisely drawn, bisymmetrical design. And the inner guard border is non-traditional. The implication may be that it was woven under some sort of controlled condition, and therefore probably for a specific cash market. There is no rule that says rugs woven for money, not that mythical idea of love, are in any way inferior. This rug has apparently hardly been exposed to sunlight, as the colors are bright, and the ivory wool is almost white.

Zeikhur 'vase' rugs seem to have come out of a long Indo-Persian tradition, but the design concept may have been directly introduced into the Caucasus through printed, painted and resist dyed cotton fabric from India re-exported from Britain (up to half of this trade was re-exported) – or by similar Persian textiles. The volume of Indian textile exports to Britain through the East India Company peaked in the late eighteenth century and declined thereafter, as British domestic productivity more than offset low Indian labor costs.[158] It is probably not a coincidence that around 1800, Transcaucasian village rug production began to grow at the same time as there was increased Indian cotton fabric export volume to Europe, and the Russians took over the Caucasian weaving areas. It is also probably no coincidence that there are no pre-nineteenth century Caucasian rugs with this design.[159]

Although the Zeikhur 'vase' design is highly stylized, the much older idea that these vases held flowers or flowering plants with green stems is carried through in this nineteenth century rug; stems and flowers in early Burhanpur textiles, for example, are placed in the same location as in Zeikhur rugs.

These vase rugs were woven mostly in long format, but occasionally in small sizes, with only one vase.

60

Size	3'3" × 6'6" (91 × 198 cm)
Warp	Z3S uniform ivory wool
Weft	Two singles, ivory wool, two shots
Knotting	V 12, H 8, 96/square inch, 1488 per dm; pile height about 3mm
Selvedges	Three pairs of reinforced warps interlaced with dark blue wool, damaged in places
Ends	Knotted meshwork with up to five rows of offset overhand knots extant, following or preceded by six rows of medium blue wool 2/1 *sumak*
Colors	7: Yellow, ivory, dark brown, medium blue, red, green, rose

Published: Spuhler et al., 1978, plate 71; Franses et al., 2017, fig. 10.11

Zeikhur tile pattern rug

The designation 'Alpan' for this type of rug may have some validity, but there is no hard evidence to confirm it. The village of Alpan is close to the town of Zeikhur, on the basis of contemporary information.[160] 'Zeikhur' rugs were apparently woven in several nearby villages in the northeast Transcaucasus and partly in Dagestan about 20 km north of Quba in the foothills of the Caucasus Mountains. It is likely that this type of rug was woven at least in part by indigenous people, in this case, Lesghis, Tabassaranis and Tsakhurs.[161] The name 'Zeikhur' may be derived from the Tsakhur ethnic group.

The so called 'Alpan' field design has a long traceable origin through several media, probably in the following sequence: unglazed tile work, then glazed decorated tile, then embroidery, and finally, rugs. Tile pattern embroideries are believed to date from as early as the late seventeenth century. It is reasonable to assume that the embroideries and the rugs come from the same region, and it is intriguing to contemplate that they might, at some point, have been produced contemporaneously. But there is no way at present to pinpoint when that could have been. The problem is that iconic embroideries are pretty conclusively thought to be from well before the nineteenth century and conventional wisdom would date this rug to the nineteenth century. Nineteenth century embroideries in this pattern are generally thought to have lost the original feeling. But maybe not. On the other hand, could there have been laid back early embroideries that served as models for Zeikhur pile rugs? Supporting this idea is the fact that somehow these embroideries have survived in numbers up to the present day.

The relatively sophisticated level of field design in Zeikhur rugs in general is noteworthy; several embroidery-sourced designs were used. Comparatively early 'Alpan' rugs like this one have elements closely spaced and are on black/brown fields, like the embroideries, or sometimes, on yellow. The spacing echoes the 'tile' embroidery original.

This rug follows the early fairly common single unit embroidery pattern fairly closely in feeling, but as a vertical repeat design. Due to the limitations of relatively coarse village weaving, the curvilinear tendril-like forms attached to the diagonal hexagonal forms in the early embroideries are reduced to claw-like forms in the rug.

It is probable that the convention of narrow loom width limited most of these rugs to a single column of ornaments, but there are a few with multiple columns of medallions and diagonal forms. They have as a model, among others, a multiple medallion embroidery in the Burns Collection.[162] One of these multiple-column nineteenth century rugs, location at this point unknown, is a yellow ground *sumak*; another is a reduced *kelleh* on black, likely not Transcaucasian. By about 1900, 4 × 5-meter *sumaks* were being produced in workshops with Zeikhur-like borders, but none has shown up with a repeat 'Alpan' pattern.

As the nineteenth century wore on, it appears that this design became more loosely drawn, with elements farther apart than in the pictured example. Sometimes, palmettes were introduced into the design, and dark blue fields were fairly common. It stands to reason that these design changes came about under the pressure of commercial production.

There is known to be at this point only one other rug almost precisely like this. It is remarkably close in color use and design, down to the little rosettes in the field, the box-like forms in the lower right and left edges of the field, and the use of a single 'barber's pole' outside guard border. It is almost half again more finely knotted, but the high density was not used to introduce more detail.[163] As with much rug weaving, high knot density may have been a selling point for some people in the business in the Caucasus.

61

Size	3'5" × 10'11" (104 × 333 cm)
Warp	Z3S uniform ivory/beige wool
Weft	Two singles, ivory, beige, brown, medium blue wool, one (rarely), two shots
Knotting	V 10, H 10, 100/square inch, 1550 per dm; pile height about 3mm
Selvedges	Three pairs of reinforced warps interlaced with medium blue wool, damaged in places
Ends	Top: remnants of knotted meshwork offset overhand knots following up to three rows of medium blue wool 2/1 *sumak*; Bottom: knotted meshwork (incomplete) with four rows of offset overhand knots, followed by five rows of medium blue wool 2/1 *sumak* (incomplete)
Colors	8: medium to dark blue, dark red to salmon, ivory, light blue, rose, green, yellow, brown (corroded)

Published: Tschebull, 1992, plate 21

Zeikhur long rug

Sometimes referred to as originating in 'Bidjov/Bijov', this pattern seems to have had its greatest, most complex development in the Zeikhur area. 'Bijov' may be a fanciful source. On Latif Kerimov-sourced maps, it is in the highlands above the Kura river valley, not very close to Zeikhur. Rugs in this particular ascending design cited as being from Bijov, are clearly cruder, and look as if they may be derivative, probably based on the Zeikhur version.

In this rug, the vertically oriented palmettes in the field, in three columns, come in several variations and are flanked by what look like curving leaf forms. Two areas in the field have a herringbone-like wave pattern, probably taken from Kurdish garden and other workshop carpets.[164] All these motifs echo earlier traditions.

It is not a great leap of faith to think that this field design is descended from sixteenth-century Ottoman *seraser* fabric on which appear stylized tulips with clasping leaves within an ogival lattice.[165] The design was picked up as a single column in at least one small ivory field Turkish village rug, gathered from a mosque in Sivrihisar.[166] Apparently a bit later it appears in a Turkish rug with three columns of palmette forms within a crude lattice on ivory,[167] also echoing the Ottoman original. The apparent first Caucasian version seems to be in workshop-produced 'shield' carpets from the northeast Transcaucasus,[168] which have horizontal rows of upward pointing palmettes flanked by bent-topped cypresses (perhaps), as Arthur Upham Pope speculated. There are other manifestations of this three-column ascending design,[169] and single column pieces, in substantially different structures.[170]

Assuming the Zeikhur design is a 'shield' carpet relative, one would like to know how the design morphed into this style of Zeikhur weaving. This 'Zeikhur/Bijov' design was quite stable over a long period (on the basis of in-woven dates, from at least 1202/1787 to the equivalent of 1879, and was probably woven contemporaneously with some 'shield' carpets. Whether the Bijov dated 1202 is reflective of when it was woven is unknowable, but the date is clearly drawn.

Many Zeikhurs in this design are dated and some have inscriptions, as this one has (but it is illegible). It is woven with very even coloration, except for the breaks in the madder and medium blue (which might have been intentional), lies perfectly flat and is very evenly and finely woven. The in-woven date 1297/1879 places this rug as well into the synthetic dye era. The implication is that at least some of these rugs were produced by accomplished weavers who used only more expensive natural dyes, perhaps on commission. Were some of the buyers local? The predominant long narrow format of most of these rugs implies that they were.

Unlike most other Caucasian village rug patterns, this one repeats its diverse group of ornaments in a single design unit repeated three and a half times along the length of field. This is the type of execution one expects to see in the best workshop carpets, woven under supervision. Yet in many cases these 'Zeikhur/Bijov' rugs, again on the basis of dated examples, were being woven before the Russians institutionalized rug weaving in the Caucasus, so workshop-style supervision was not generally likely. In addition, the narrow format would have made such supervision uneconomic, as at most, two weavers worked on a rug like this.

62

Size	2'9" × 4'8" (84 × 142 cm)
Warp	Z3S dark gray, 10% ivory wool
Weft	Two singles, brown, orange, ivory wool, two shots
Knotting	V 12, H 7, 84/square inch, 1302 per dm; pile height about 4mm
Selvedges	Three pairs of reinforced warps interlaced with medium to dark blue wool, ½"/1.5 cm in orange
Ends	Top: two rows of medium blue wool 2/1 *sumak* followed by a warp fringe; Bottom: remnants of knotted meshwork with up to four rows of offset overhand knots, followed by two rows of medium blue wool 2/1 *sumak*
Colors	9: ivory, orange, blue green, dark blue, golden brown, medium blue, salmon, yellow, dark brown/black (uncorroded to slightly corroded)

Published: Landreau, 1978, plate 45; HALI 62, 1992, plate 6

Zeikhur rug

This piece has all the typical structural characteristics of old Zeikhur pile rugs, and the borders are conventional, but it is somehow different. For one thing, the warps are dark gray, as opposed to the more common use of relatively uniform ivory. Although not apparent in the illustration, the rug's curvature is also unusual; most Zeikhurs are straight and lie flat, a mark of relatively sophisticated weaving. The out of the norm field design, a single column of diamond-shaped forms topped by a rosette, is likely derived from the same basic slit-tapestry *kilim* source as the Shirvan fragment in Plate 46.

Caucasian rugs are almost never one-off examples – the weaving culture was apparently too conservative for that to happen. But this one might be, with its ivory field, small size and varied and unusual filler motifs, including 'endless knots' – or is it a lone survivor of a type, and might be quite an old rug? More sophisticated fiber tests may, at some point, provide an answer.

From personal observation, it seems probable that older Zeikhurs have more red dyes at the yellow end of the spectrum.

63

Size	4'7" × 3'4" (140 × 102 cm)
Warp	Z2S ivory wool
Weft	Z2S black/dark brown wool, 4 shots
Knotting	V 4, H 8, 32/square inch, 496 per dm; pile height about 8mm
Selvedges	None, but, based on conventions with regard to how borders in coarse Transcaucasian pile rugs are woven, only the selvedge is missing
Ends	Missing
Colors	8: red, yellow, pale yellow, ivory, dark brown (undyed), aubergine, medium blue, light blue

Zaqatal rug fragment

This fragment is certainly stunning, at least to its owner, because of the quartered diamonds between the 'Memling'-guls, which give the feeling of two patterns in the same space; the varied use of color in the layout; the simple reciprocal border; the horizontal 'barber's pole' stripes across the field between the guls, and the two yellows. And because it is possible, because it appears that only the selvedge on the right side is missing (there are weft returns), to determine the original width of the rug. It was about 4'11" (150 cm) wide, and given its modular design, could have been any length, but was probably 7 (213 cm) to 8 (244 cm) feet long. Not having the whole rug is not a serious hinderance to enjoyment.

Based on ethnographic data, it is likely that this type of rug was woven by indigenous people, in this case, Avars and Tsakhurs. Many such pieces have a 'Memling-gul' pattern, but not exactly like the fragment.

It is clear that the wefts here are Z2S, which produces a thicker structure, but in a coarse rug like this it does not seem to matter. Knotting density is variable.

Fragmented rugs like this are the type of textile that one could see on Turkish mosque floors, and it is possible that this is a mosque fragment.[171] There was at one time in the 1990s, a mosque in Zaqatal that contained pile rugs in this weave. Perhaps this fragment is from there. It is said to have come out of the Caucasus post-1991.

Endnotes

1 For rug and textile classification, Robert Pinner, by training a metallurgist, popularized this term in the 1970s to describe the structure of a weaving and the materials used. It is, as almost everything Pinner wrote or talked about, quite precise.

2 Atkin 1980, p. XI.

3 There is a whole non-Turkmen culture of 'bedding' bags, most of which are pile-woven and some in what can be described as being at least partially in a '*sumak*' weft-wrapping technique, which may well be defined using different terminology.

4 Housego 1978, pp. 42–44.

5 For a cogent essay on felt origins and use, see Veronika Gervers, 'Felt in Eurasia', in Landreau 1978, pp. 16–22.

6 Mallett 2000.

7 For approximate conversion to imperial measure: kilometers to miles multiply by 0.6; meters to feet, multiply by 3.3.

8 Bozgush, also Bozkush, Bozghush, Bozqush: Manouchehr Haghighat in Tehran, an Iranian friend with family connections to East Azarbayjan, prefers Bozgush. I am told it is a Turkic term, *boz* (gray), *gush/kush* (bird).

9 Richard Tapper, personal communication.

10 Housego 1978, p.43.

11 The MFA, Boston is a good source.

12 Re stucco see Grabar & Hill 1967; re derivation from script, see Julia Bailey, 'Carpets and Kufesque', in Thompson, Shaffer & Mildh 2010, pp.18–29.

13 A village allegedly near Heriz named Barjid is cited as a source of rugs with structure and coloration very similar to that of export-oriented, cotton-foundation Qarajehs, but using a Transcaucasian pattern called 'Chelaberd'. However, the village name was never mentioned by the Iranians with whom I thoroughly visited the area, nor is it included in Cecil Edwards' baseline book on Iranian rugs, or on his maps, and does not turn up on Google Maps. The use of a popular Transcaucasian village pattern used relatively late in East Azarbayjani rural rug production smacks suspiciously of introduction by bazaaris – somewhere.

14 For more on Qarajeh, see Tschebull 1997(b).

15 Marla Mallett: 'The problem could be in the warping process itself, it could be different warp yarns used toward one side (with a slightly different spin or ply) or could be a difference in the way the weaving proceeded, with two weavers packing their wefts differently. Changes to more modern loom types could minimize these problems.'

16 For more on the subject see Tschebull 1995.

17 Meister & Azadi 1971, pl. 46.

18 Tschebull 2001 (ICOC lecture, Milan 1999).

19 E.g., Burns 2002, pl. 3.

20 For more on this pattern and 'Heriz' export weaving in general, see Tschebull 1997(b).

21 Herrmann 1989, pl. 24, 5'6" × 7'4", 1800 k/dm².

22 Schürmann 1965, pl. 62.

23 Herrmann 1985, pl. 46, 1470 k/dm². For a very similar rug, Burns 2011, pl. 8, 2604 k/dm², the cited knot count has probably been doubled, as it falls well outside the norm.

24 Plates 19, 43, 47, and 48 were exhibited from 9 October 2014 to 9 March 2015 in 'Flat Weaves from the Collection of Raoul Tschebull' at the Museum of Fine Arts, Boston.

25 Parviz Tanavoli, personal communication, but also in Tanavoli 1985.

26 Somewhat similar *gilims* appear in Sadighi & Vok 1996, plate 46, and Herrmann 1991, plate 35, and there was a red, green and blue zig-zag design Qarabaghi/Kazak piece in the Istanbul market some years ago. For an estimable Anatolian parallel in the Harry Koll Collection, see HALI 173, p.123.

27 Sadighi & Vok 1996, pl. 46.

28 Sadighi & Vok 1996, dated pieces, pls. 57, 60.

29 Sadighi & Hawkes 2014, pls. 47–54.

30 Metropolitan Museum of Art, New York, 66.173.

31 Istanbul University Library, F. 1422, folio 24a.

32 For more on *jajims*, see 'Why Warp-Faced Covers are Collectible', 14 November 2009, Rug and Textile Morning, at the Textile Museum, Washington, D.C., *https//rjohnhowe.wordpress.com/2009/12/30/why-warp-faced-covers-are-collectible/*.

33 Tanavoli 1985, pl. 279, attributes a similar sized *jajim* with similar colors to Moghan Shahsavan and thinks it was intended to be a camel cover.

34 Marla Mallett, private correspondence.

35 Tanavoli 1985, pl. 37.

36 Metropolitan Museum of Art, New York, 17.190.724.

37 By way of comparison, the panel width in this piece, with two contrasting warp-substitution designs, narrow guard borders, and two plainweave stripes, is 23 cm wide, while in a larger *jajim* with a very similar design, Sadighi & Vok 1996, pl. 73, individual panels with one design and one plainweave stripe are 21 cm wide.

38 Parviz Tanavoli, private correspondence.

39 Parviz Tanavoli, private correspondence, says that plate 31 in Tanavoli 1985 is the true *yaddi qardash* pattern and that this piece is not the same. Any difference in design may simply relate to time and place. The Azarbayjani *jajim* labelled *yaddi qardash* in Sadighi & Vok 1996, pl. 73, is also slightly different from Tanavoli's plate 31. These weavers were pretty good artists, and each likely put her own personality into these *jajims*.

40 Wertime, Wright & Merritt 1992.

41 Wright & Wertime 1995, pl. XII.

42 Kirchheim et al. 1993, pls. 42, 49, 50.

43 Gentle abrasion from use knocks some of the scales off wool fiber, which helps to produce luster if the wool was high quality and well sorted in the first place.

44 Spurr 2018.

45 Spurr 1999.

46 Bob Mann in conversation.

47 Misinformation dates back a long way: Coxon 1884, p.53, thinks he is buying some village rugs in Baku that are 150 years old – pretty clearly not true, too early – and he illustrates a pile rug he attributes to Dagestan, which is much more likely from the western Transcaucasus.

48 Michael Bischof, personal communication.

49 E.g.: McMullan 1965, pl.108; HALI 158, cover; Kirchheim et al. 1993, pls. 82, 83. The last have Turkmen gul-like medallions and pendants like early Lori Pambak Kazaks, but no animal forms, and the gul shape is lost. Both are probably from the same workshop.

50 Elena Tsareva, personal communication.

51 Rippon Boswell, Wiesbaden, 21 November 1998, lot 189. This design has several iterations. In a Bud Holland-sourced embroidery at Sotheby's New York, 31 January 2014, lot 1, the green bird forms in the rug are replaced in the almost square red medallion by serrated diamond/palmette forms somewhat like those seen in the RB embroidery, but its pendant palmettes are replaced by cartouche-like forms. It seems clear that there is not always a straight line of development between animal art and floral art; the two embroideries cited here are dated to the same period, although the second one is in 'stem stitch'. Rug designs related to embroideries seem derivative, simplified, but the real issue is that village weaving was in a much more restrictive medium, which required reduction of detail that could be achieved with embroidery.

52 It is possible that most of these 'Caucasian' embroideries were created as decorative quilt tops that did not get damaged in use as they were strictly for show and were treasured and therefore available as models for 19th century rug designs, as well as for current day collectors. I have seen enough embroideries with little bits of dark cotton thread hanging off the back to make me at least suspect I am right. Access to a good time machine would be helpful.

53 Franses et al. 2017, fig. 10.6.

54 Rippon Boswell, Wiesbaden, 18 November 1995, lot 114. Consigned by Günther and Ingrid Rapp from Oldenburg, Germany, who bought it from Bausback in Mannheim. I first saw it in about 1975 in Frankfurt.

55 Grogan, Boston, 20 November 2016, Rudnick Collection, lot 57.

56 For an expansion of this idea, see Tschebull 1978(c).

57 Lefevre 1977, pl. 14.

58 Bennett 1981, pl. 5.

59 Ibid, pl. 8.

60 Herrmann 1991, pl. 13.

61 Bornoutian 1976, describing the ethnic/religious makeup of the Khanate, population movements after the Russian takeover, and the 1829–32 census conducted by Ivan Shopen.

62 Lefevre 1977, p. 48.

63 Kaffel 1998, pl. 19. For other relatively early dated examples, see Herrmann 1989, pl. 15, a Kazak prayer rug dated 1866–67; Kaffel 1998, p. 13, which has an in-woven date that has been read as 1245/1829.

64 Jeff Spurr, in conversation.

65 Walter Denny's opinion applied to other Caucasian rug designs.

66 E.g., Tschebull 1971, pl. 29; McMullan 1965, pl. 49; Bennett 1981, pl. 16; Herrmann 1985, pl. 28; Keshishian 1992, pl. 4; and several others in private collections and dealers' inventory.

67 McMullan 1965, pl. 49 has Ponceau 2R-dyed wefts, and a row of likely Ponceau pile removed. See also Tschebull 1979. Tschebull 1971, pl. 30, is a prayer rug likely from the same village and also has Ponceau in it.

68 Keshishian 1992, pl. 4.

69 Herrmann 1985, pl. 28.

70 Herrmann 1992, pl. 38. The text for Herrmann 1985, pl. 28, also cites an unattributed prayer rug with an in-woven date of 1283/1866.

71 E.g., Grogan, Boston, 20 November 2016, Rudnick Collection, lot 94.

72 Tschebull 1978(c).

73 The design is described as a 'double inverted keyhole' by Michael Franses. Zick 1961, in an article on the 'Bellini' design development in Anatolia, traces the rug design evolution in stages from the end of the fifteenth century and cites rugs in relevant European paintings.

74 Walter Denny, personal communication.

75 E.g., TIEM 343, Ölçer & Denny, 1999, pl. 11.

76 Hovanissian 1971.

77 There is a variety of weft colors, and a highly variable number of ground wefts, as well as heavy weft cables used to correct curvature, all indicating that this weaving was not produced under controlled conditions.

78 Tschebull 1971, pl. 23.

79 Dmitriev 2001: 'Nomadic dwellings', L. Slastnikova, pp.72–77; 'Felt and Felt Articles', E. Selinenkova, pp. 207–211.

80 Grogan, Boston, 20 November 2016, Rudnick Collection, lot 83.

81 Fred and Susan Ingham Collection, exhibited at ACOR in Seattle, 2004.

82 Sotheby's New York, 31 January 2014, lot 47; Herrmann 1993, pl. 53; Bennett 1981, pl. 39.

83 E.g., Tschebull 1971, pl. 12.

84 Elena Tsareva in conversation.

85 Lefevre and Partners, London, 3 February 1978, lot 43.

86 Wright & Wertime 1995, pl. 33, p. 86.

87 E.g., Bennett & Bassoul 2003, pl. 38; this example has fewer colors and is slightly more mechanical in drawing than the yellow-field pieces.

88 Vügar Dadaşov, private correspondence; also see *www.azerbaijanrugs.com*.

89 Hasson 1986, pl. 11.

90 Hagop Manoyan, in conservation, has commented on the scarcity of these weavings.

91 LeFevre/The Persian Carpet Galleries, London, 17 May 1974, lot 45, missing outer guard border.

92 Tschebull 1971, pl. 40.

93 Spurr 2018, pp.98–109.

94 It makes one think of the cathedral cut into the Mesquita in Cordoba.

95 E.g., Herrmann 1988, pl. 32.

96 Keshishian 1992, pl. 41.

97 For an additional color illustration of this type of sumak bag, see Wertime 1998, pl.60, where another source detailing the design origin of 'marching peacocks' is described.

98 For another version of this one-eyed open-mouthed creature see Landreau & Pickering 1969, pl. 43.

99 Böhmer 2003, pp. 207–208.

100 E.g., *http//www.zeller.de/de/katalog/auktion-112-april-2012/auktionsartikel/konja-11/*.

101 Azadi et al. 2001, pl. 205.

102 Email correspondence from Rema Zenyalova at the Azerbaijan National Carpet Museum.

103 TIEM 172, Yetkin 1978, Vol. 1, pl. 40, also pl. 38.

104 Kirchheim et al. 1993, pl. 8.

105 E.g., Herrmann 1990, pl. 22.

106 Sotheby's, New York, 11 June 2008, lot 101 = HALI 158, 2008, p. 135.

107 MMA, New York, 1972.80.2.

108 John Douglass, 'Connoisseur's Choice', HALI 57, 1990, pp. 94–95; Eiland 1990, pl. 171, where it is said to have wool wefts.

109 Christie's, London, 19 April 2016, lot 20, for which the auction cataloguing confirms white cotton wefting.

110 Textile Museum, R36.5.1; see Tschebull 1971, pl. 7.

111 Herrmann 1992, pl. 43.

112 Sadighi & Vok 1996, pl. 79.

113 See also Stanzer et al. 1986, pl. 79, which has the exact same layout, but with some brocaded forms, and Ampe 1994, plate 26. The latter piece is especially good looking, with lots of brocading. A slightly different, but surely related version appears in an advertisement for Galerie Sailer, HALI 65, 1992, pp. 60–61.

114 Marla Mallett website, *Woven Structures Update*: 'The loom was warped with wide solid stripes of varying colors that matched a majority of the intended wefts; thus the weaver avoided the speckled look of exposed light warp yarns.'

115 Vügar Dadaşov, private correspondence; see *www.azerbaijanrugs.com.*

116 Jeff Spurr, in conversation.

117 Probably the best looking of these *kilims*, in The Textile Museum, Washington, DC, is illustrated in color in Landreau & Pickering 1969, pl. 1. It has more palmettes, is less geometricized, better spaced, and with a greater range of colors than the norm.

118 A good old example of this type, but with two rows of palmettes and conventional pile rug borders is illustrated in Herrmann 1993, pl.28; also in prayer configuration, Kaffel 1998, pl. 76.)

119 Petsopoulos 1979, pp. 238–246 and pl.280.

120 For the slit-tapestry version, see McMullan & Reichert, n.d., pl. 25. McMullan catalogued the *kilim* as Turkish, but had an inkling, in the last paragraph of the plate description, that it was Caucasian.

121 E.g., Thompson & Farnham 2008, pl. 77; Sotheby's New York, 31 January 2014, lot 152; Schürmann 1964, pl. 80.

122 E.g., Vakıflar Museum, Istanbul, No E-1; Balpinar & Hirsch 1988, pl.7.

123 Parviz Tanavoli in conversation.

124 This type of Caucasian rug is featured in Tschebull 2008.

125 Private collection (sold by Hagop Manoyan), 3'3" × 10'0"; Herrmann 1984, pl. 33, has outside guard border at the top of the rug only; and a red field fragment, seen at Hagop Manoyan, New York.

126 Rippon Boswell, Wiesbaden, Spring 2001, lot 62; Ampe 1994, pl. 45.

127 Private collection, Connecticut; Christie's London, 7 October 2014, lot 55.

128 Thompson & Farnham, pl. 75.

129 For more on this subject, see Willem Floor, 'The Import of Indian Textiles into Safavid Persia', in Thompson, Shaffer and Mildh 2010, pp.186–204.

130 Spurr 2018. For additional information on relevant trade flows, see Broadberry & Gupta 2005, which describes with voluminous data how the East India Company's Indian textile imports peaked at the end of the eighteenth century and that almost half of them were re-exported. It seems logical that at least some of this bounty was re-exported to Baku.

131 Erdmann 1970, p. 174.

132 Herrmann 1986, pl. 34.

133 No. 62-1229. Kuba Perepedil prayer rug, dated 1272/1855, wool warp, undyed cotton weft; symmetrically knotted wool pile, knotted fringes, 148 × 111 cm, 1540k/dm^2.

134 Kaffel 1998, description to pl. 47

135 Kaffel 1998, pls. 47–50; see also Stanzer et al. 1986, pl. 57.

136 Christine Klose, 'The Perepedil Enigma', HALI 55, 1991, pp.110–17.

137 Burns 1987, pl. 20.

138 Tschebull 1971, pl. 7.

139 Among others: Herrmann 1982, pl. 19; Bennett 1981, pl. 200; Burns 2011, pl. 24.

140 See Brüggemann & Böhmer 1983, pl. 36.

141 Lefevre, London, 26 May 1978, color plate 8, claimed to be from the Transcaucasus and eighteenth century, which is possible.

142 Michael Bischof, private correspondence.

143 Wendel Swan, private correspondence.

144 For an almost lookalike example, see Yohe & Jones 1968, pl. 86. See also Spuhler, König & Volkmann 1978, pl. 33.

145 Vakıflar A305, 150 × 240 cm, found in Divriği by Ellis and Denny in 1975. Balpinar & Hirsch 1988, pl.3, pp. 182–183.

146 Brüggemann & Böhmer 1983, pl. 54.

147 See Plate 32 for more on this move of design from nomads to settled weavers.

148 Marla Mallett defines this technically as '...because the weavers failed to add the extra weft ease that was proper'.

149 Vügar Dadaşov, personal communication.

150 Bennett 1981, pl. 356.

151 Ibid, pl. 358.

152 See Plate 24 for an explanation of the probable origin of this design concept.

153 Wright & O'Bannon 1980.

154 Such as a carpet formerly in the Erich Maria Remarque Collection.

155 One example, now in an American private collection, is illustrated in Schürmann 1964, pl. 114.

156 For example, large sumaks illustrated by Schürmann, 1964, pl. 120, and Lefevre, 4 March 1983, lot 40, plus a pile rug, Kirchheim et al. 1993, pl. 60. All appear to be nineteenth century weavings.

157 McMullan 1965, pl. 27.

158 Broadberry and Gupta 2005 .

159 For more detail and color illustrations of some of the pieces cited, see Tschebull 1992, pp. 83–95.

160 Vügar Dadaşov, personal communication.

161 See Geiger 1959, for detail.

162 Burns 1987, pl. 49.

163 Tschebull 1992, pl. 17.

164 E.g., McMullan 1965, pl. 28.

165 E.g., Metropolitan Museum of Art, New York, 52.20.19. A further stylized version is MMA 52.20.15. Thanks to Jeff Spurr who helped me to see this relationship.

166 TIEM 310, eighteenth century (?), Ölçer & Denny 1999, pl. 84.

167 Kirchheim et al. 1993, pl. 62.

168 Pinner & Franses, 1978.

169 Including, for example, Schürmann 1964, pls. 6 and 94.

170 Kirchheim et al. 1993, pl. 61.

171 Hazledine 1994, pp.94–95.

Bibliography

Altstadt, Audrey L., *The Azerbaijani Turks, Power and Identity under Russian Rule*, Hoover Institution Press, Stanford, 1992

Ampe, Patrick, and Rie Ampe, *Textielkunst, een persoonlijke keunze*, Kailash Gallery, Antwerp, 1994

Atkin, Muriel, *Russia and Iran, 1780–1828*, University of Minnesota Press, Minneapolis, 1980

Avery, Peter, Gavin Hambly and Charles Melville (eds), 'The tribes in eighteenth and nineteenth century Iran', in *From Nadir Shah to the Islamic Republic,* The Cambridge History of Iran, Vol. 7, Cambridge University Press, 1991

Azadi, Siawosch, and Peter Alford Andrews, *Mafrash. Woven transport packs as an art form among the Shahsevan and other nomads in Persia*, Dietrich Reimer Verlag + Weltkunst Verlag, Berlin, 1985

Azadi, Siawosch U., Kerimov, Latif, and Werner Zollinger, *Azerbaijani-Caucasian Rugs*, Paul Hartung, Hamburg, 2001

Balpınar, Belkıs, and Udo Hirsch, *Carpets of the Vakıflar Museum Istanbul*. Uta Hülsey Verlag, Wesel, 1988

Bennett, Ian, *Oriental Rugs, Volume 1, Caucasian*, Oriental Textile Press, London, 1981

Bennett, lan, and Aziz Bassoul, *Tapis du Caucase/Rugs of the Caucasus*, Nicolas Sursock Museum, Beirut 2003

Böhmer, Harald, *Koekboya, Natural Dyes and Textiles. A colour journey from Turkey to India and beyond*, REMHÖB-Verlag, Ganderkesee, 2002

Bornoutian, George, *Eastern Armenia on the Eve of the Russian Conquest: The Khanate of Erevan under the Governorship of Hoseyn Qoli Khan Qajar*, 1807–1827, Ph.D. thesis, University of California, Los Angeles, 1976

Broadberry, Stephen N., and Bishnupriya Gupta, *Cotton Textiles and the Great Divergence: Lancashire, India and Shifting Competitive Advantage, 1600–1850*. CEPR (UK) Discussion Paper No. 5183, August 2005. https://ssrn.com/abstract=790866

Brüggemann, Werner, and Harald Böhmer, *Rugs of the Peasants and Nomads of Anatolia*, Kunst & Antiquitäten, Munich, 1983

Bunn, Stephanie, *Nomadic Felts*, British Museum Press, London, 2010

Burns, James D., *The Caucasus: Traditions in Weaving*, Court Street Press, Seattle, 1987

Burns, James D., *Antique Rugs of Kurdistan. A Historical Legacy of Woven Art*, Textile and Art Publications, London, 2002

Burns, James D., *Visions of Nature. The Antique Weavings of Persia*, Umbra Editions, New York, 2011

Coxon, Herbert, *Oriental Carpets; How They Are Made and Conveyed to Europe, with a Narrative of a Journey to the East in Search of Them*, T. Fisher Unwin, London, 1884

Cloudman, Ruth H., *A Rich Inheritance. Oriental Rugs of the 19th and Early 20th Centuries*, Joslyn Art Museum, Omaha, 1974

Denny, Walter B., *Oriental Rugs*, Smithsonian Institution, Washington DC, 1979

Dmitriev, Vladimir, et al., *Kaukasische Volkeren/The Caucasian Peoples,* Hessenhuis, Antwerp, 2001

Eiland, Murray, *Oriental Rugs from Pacific Collections, San Francisco Bay Area Rug Society, San Francisco, 1990*

Erdmann, Kurt, *Seven Hundred Years of Oriental Carpets*, University of California Press, Los Angeles, 1970.

Franses, Michael, et.al., *Stars of the Caucasus: Silk Embroideries from Azerbaijan*, Hali Publications/Azerbaijan Ministry of Culture, London 2017

Franses, Michael, and Robert Pinner, 'Caucasian Rugs in the Victoria and Albert Museum. The Caucasian Collection', HALI 3/2, London, 1980, pp.96–115

Geiger, Bernhard, et al., *The Caucasus*, 2 Vols., Human Relations Area Files, New Haven, 1956

Geiger, Bernhard, et al., *Peoples and Languages of the Caucasus; A Synopsis*, Mouton & Co., The Hague, 1959

Grabar, Oleg, and Derek Hill, *Islamic Architecture and its Decoration, AD 800–1500*, University of Chicago Press, Chicago, 1964

Grogan & Company auction catalog, *The Rosalie and Mitchell Rudnick Collection of Caucasian Rugs*, Boston, 20 November 2016

Hasson, Rachel, *Caucasian Rugs*, L.A. Mayer Memorial Institute for Islamic Art, Jerusalem, 1986

Hazledine, Tony, 'The Mosque Rugs of Zalatala,' HALI 78, 1994, pp. 94–95

Herrmann, Eberhart, *Seltene Orientteppiche V*, Munich, 1983

Herrmann, Eberhart, *Seltene Orientteppiche VI*, Munich, 1984

Herrmann, Eberhart, *Seltene Orientteppiche VII*, Munich, 1985

Herrmann, Eberhart, *Seltene Orientteppiche VIII*, Munich, 1986

Herrmann, Eberhart, *Seltene Orientteppiche X*, Munich, 1988

Hermann, Eberhart, *Asiatische Teppich- und Textilkunst 1*, Munich, 1989

Hermann, Eberhart, *Asiatische Teppich- und Textilkunst 2*, Munich, 1990

Hermann, Eberhart, *Asiatische Teppich- und Textilkunst 3*, Munich, 1991

Hermann, Eberhart, *Asiatische Teppich- und Textilkunst 4*, Munich, 1992

Herrmann, Eberhart, *Kaukasische Teppichkunst im 19. Jahrhundert, Ein Bilderbuch*, Munich, 1993

Housego, Jenny, 'Part I', in Landreau, Anthony N. (ed.), *Yörük, The Nomadic Weaving Tradition of the Middle East*, Pittsbugh, Carnegie Museum of Art, 1978

Hovanissian, Richard, *Republic of Armenia*, University of California Press, Berkeley, 1971

Kaffel, Ralph, *Caucasian Prayer Rugs*, Lawrence King/Hali Publications, London, 1998

Kaffel, Ralph, 'Ivory, Black & Gold: Marasali Prayer Rugs', HALI 103, 1999, pp. 82–91

Kerimov, Latif, et al., *Rugs & Carpets from the Caucasus: The Russian Collections*, Aurora, Leningrad, 1984

Keshishian, Harold M., *The Treasure of the Caucasus. Rugs from American Collections*. Near Eastern Art Research Center, Washington, 1992

King, Charles, *The Ghost of Freedom, A History of the Caucasus*, Oxford University Press, New York, 2008

Kirchheim, Heinrich, et al., *Orient Stars, A Carpet Collection*, Hali Publications, London, 1993

Klose, Christine, 'The Perepedil Enigma', HALI 55, 1991, pp. 110–117

Landreau, Anthony N., ed., *Yörük, The Nomadic Weaving Tradition of the Middle East*, Carnegie Museum of Art, Pittsbugh, 1978

Landreau, Anthony N. and W. R. Pickering, *From the Bosporus to Samarkand. Flat-Woven Rugs*, The Textile Museum, Washington, D.C., 1969

Lefevre, Jean, *Caucasian Carpets*, Lefevre & Partners, London, 1977

Mallett, Marla, *Woven Structures. A Guide to Oriental Rug and Textile Analysis*, Christopher Publications, Atlanta, 2000

McMullan, Joseph V., *Islamic Carpets*, Near Eastern Art Research Center, New York, 1965

McMullan Joseph V., and Donald O. Reichert, *The George Walter Vincent and Belle Townsley Smith Collection of Islamic Rugs*, Springfield, MA, n.d.

Meister, Peter Wilhelm, and Siawosch Azadi, *Persische Teppiche*, Museum Für Kunst und Gewerbe, Hamburg, and Museum für Kunsthandwerk, Frankfurt, Hamburg 1971

Ölçer, Nazan, and Walter B. Denny, *Anatolian Carpets. Masterpieces from The Museum of Turkish and Islamic Arts*, Istanbul, Ertuğ & Kocabıyık, Berne, 1999

Petsopoulos, Yanni, *Kilims*, Thames and Hudson, London, 1979

Pinner, Robert, and Michael Franses, 'Caucasian "Shield" Carpets', HALI 1/1, 1978, pp.4–22

Sadighi, Hamid, and Ignazio Vok, *Vok Collection, Caucasus Persia*, Edition Vok, Munich, 1996

Sadighi, Hamid, and Karin Hawkes, *Kelims und andere Flachgewebe aus der Sammlung Neiriz / Kilims and Other Flatweaves from the Neiriz Collection*, Wasmuth, Halle/Saale, 2014

Selinenkova, E., 'Felt and Felt Articles', in Dmitriev, Vladimir, et al., *Kaukasische volkeren/The Caucasian Peoples* Hessenhuis, Antwerp, 2011, pp. 207–211

Schürmann, Ulrich, *Caucasian Rugs*, Klinkhart & Bierman, Braunschweig, 1965

Shelley, Louise, and Richard E. Wright, 'Caucasian Rugs in the late Nineteenth Century', HALI 3/1, 1980, pp. 3–7

Slastnikova, L., 'Nomadic Dwellings', in Dmitriev, Vladimir, et al., *Kaukasische volkeren/The Caucasian Peoples* Hessenhuis, Antwerp, 2011, pp. 72–77

Spuhler, Friedrich, Hans König, and Martin Volkmann, *Alte Orientteppiche: Meisterstücke aus deutschen Privatsammlungen*, Callwey Verlag, Munich, 1978

Spurr, Jeff, 'Revisiting the Shahsavan', HALI 104, 1999, pp.19–55

Spurr, Jeff, 'Marasali — The Kashmir Connection', HALI 105, 1999, pp.75–77

Spurr, Jeff, 'Creative Encounters. Kashmir shawl imagery in Caucasian rug design', HALI 198, 2018, pp.98–109

Stanzer, Wilfried, et al., *Antique Oriental Carpets from Austrian Collections*, TKF, Vienna, 1986

Stone, Peter F., *Rugs of the Caucasus: Structure and Design*, Chicago, 1984

Tanavoli, Parviz, *Shahsavan, Iranian Rugs and Textiles*, Rizzoli, New York, 1985

Tapper, Richard, 'Shahsevan in Safavid Persia', *Bulletin of The School of Oriental and African Studies* 37, London, 1974, pp. 321–354

Tapper, Richard, *Pasture and Politics: Economics, Conflict and Ritual among Shahsevan Nomads of Northwestern Iran*, Academic Press, London, 1979

Tapper, Richard, 'One hump or two? Hybrid camels and pastoral cultures', *Production Pastorale et Societe* 16, 1985, pp. 55–69

Tapper, Richard, 'Raiding, reaction and rivalry: Shahsevan tribes in the constitutional period', *Bulletin of The School of Oriental and African Studies* 49, London, 1986, pp. 508–531

Tapper, Richard, *Frontier Nomads of Iran, A political and social history of the Shahsevan*, Cambridge University Press, Cambridge, 1997

Tapper, Richard, and Jon Thompson, eds., *The Nomadic Peoples of Iran*, Azimuth Editions, London, 2002

Thompson, Jon and Thomas J. Farnham, *Timbuktu to Tibet: Exotic Rugs and Textiles from New York Collectors*, The Hajji Baba Club, New York, 2008

Thompson, Jon, Daniel Shaffer, and Pirjetta Mildh, eds., *Carpets and Textiles in the Iranian World, 1400–1700*, The May Beattie Archive, Ashmolean Museum, and The Bruschettini Foundation for Islamic and Asian Art, Oxford and Genoa, 2010

Tschebull, Raoul, *Kazak. Carpets of the Caucasus*, Near Eastern Art Research Center/New York Rug Society, New York, 1971(a)

Tschebull, Raoul, 'Kazak Rugs', *The Textile Museum Journal*, Washington, DC, Vol. 3, No. 2, 1971(b), pp. 2–5

Tschebull, Raoul, 'Northwestern Iran and the Transcaucasus, Part II', in Landreau, Anthony N. (ed.), *Yörük, The Nomadic Weaving Tradition of the Middle East*, Carnegie Museum of Art, Pittsburgh, 1978(a)

Tschebull, Raoul E, 'Antique Lori Pile Weaving', HALI 1/1, 1978(b), pp. 26–28

Tschebull, Raoul, 'The Development of four Kazak Designs', HALI 1/3, 1978(c), pp. 257–261

Tschebull, Raoul, 'Methods of dating Caucasian village and nomad rugs', HALI 2/3, 1979, pp. 218–221

Tschebull, Raoul, 'Chodor Carpets with the Tauk Nuska Göl and a Related Example', HALI 3/2, 1980, pp. 91–94.

Tschebull, Raoul, 'Zeikhur', HALI 62 , 1992, pp. 84–95

Tschebull, Raoul, 'Craft and Commerce. An Unusual Pilewoven Khorjin'. HALI 75, 1994, pp. 66–67

Tschebull, Raoul, 'Sarab' HALI 79, 1995, pp. 88–97

Tschebull, Raoul, 'Iran's Rug Forum', HALI 90, 1997(a), p. 57

Tschebull, Raoul, 'Heriz: A Historical Perspective', HALI 90, 1997(b), pp. 64–73

Tschebull, Raoul, 'Zakatala Kelleh', HALI 91, 1997(c), p.167

Tschebull, Raoul, 'Postcard from Iran: East Azarbayjan, August 1997', HALI 96, 1998, p.73

Tschebull, Raoul, 'Fieldwork in Azarbayjan', in Murray L. Eiland. Jr. and Robert Pinner, eds., *Oriental Carpet and Textile Studies VI*, Danville, 2001, pp.110–114

Tschebull, Raoul, *To Have and to Hold; Art and Function in Transport and Storage Bags. An Exhibition of Bags from New England Rug Society Members' Collections*, Boston, 2004. http://www.ne-rugsociety.org/gallery/bags/index.htm

Tschebull, Raoul, 'The Overlooked and the Under-Appreciated, Reflections on a Carpet from the South of Persia', *Ghereh* 43, Turin 2007(a), pp. 92–93

Tschebull, Raoul, 'Islands of Pile in a Sea of Flatweaves', HALI 152, 2007(b), pp. 110–11

Tschebull, Raoul E., 'Two Karagashli Rugs', HALI 156, 2008, pp. 38–39

Tschebull, Raoul, 'Beats hunting and fishing', HALI 163, 2010 (b), pp. 66–73

Tschebull, Raoul, 'Chahar Mahal Jajim', HALI 164, 2010(b), p. 27

Tschebull, Raoul E., 'An Early Kazak Rug', HALI 181, 2014, pp. 44–45

Tschebull, Raoul, and Murray Lee Eiland III, 'Trade and Change', HALI 84, 1996, pp.151–52

Wertime, John T., *Sumak Bags of Northwest Persia & Transcaucasia*, Lawrence King/Hali Publications, London, 1998

Wertime, John T., Richard E. Wright, and Jane L. Merrritt, 'Three Silk Jajims: A Case Study of a Transcaucasian Silk Project', HALI 63, 1992, pp. 72–83

Wright, Richard E., and George W. O'Bannon, *Rugs and Flatweaves of the Transcaucasus*, Pittsburgh, 1980

Wright, Richard E, *The Richard E. Wright Research Reports, A Compilation of Notes Concerning the Nature and Origins of Textiles*, 1993–2019. http://richardewright.com/

Wright, Richard E., and John T. Wertime, *Caucasian Carpets and Covers, The Weaving Culture*, Hali Publications, London, 1995

Yetkin, Şerare, *Early Caucasian Carpets in Turkey*, Vol. 1, Oguz Press, London, 1978

Yohe, Ralph, and H. McCoy Jones, *Turkish Rugs*, Washington Hajji Baba Society, Washington, D.C., 1968

Zick, Johanna, 'Eine Gruppe Von Gebetsteppichen Und Ihre Datierung', *Berichte Aus Den Ehem. Preussischen Kunstsammlungen – Neue Folge*, Berliner Museen, 1961

QARAJEH TO QUBA
Rugs and Flatweaves from East Azarbayjan and the Transcaucasus

ISBN 978-1-898113-61-4

Produced in the United Kingdom by HALI Publications Ltd., 8 Ability Plaza, Arbutus Street, London E84DT

Edited by Daniel Shaffer, Ben Evans

Designed by Misha Anikst and Ben Strachan, Anikst Design Ltd., London

Photography by Don Tuttle, Emeryville, California
Additional photography (pp. 140–1, 246–7) by Robert Puglisi, New York
East Azarbayjan field photographs (1997, 1998) © Raoul E. Tschebull

Printed and bound by Graphicom, Vicenza, Italy

The Cover
Detail of Plate 20, Azarbayjani nomad (?) warp-faced *jajim*

The Author
Born ten miles west of Manhattan, Raoul ('Mike') Tschebull grew up with his family's unusual old oriental rugs, puzzled over them, had trouble figuring out where and when they were woven. It produced a lifelong interest. As a result, he has been a long-term collector of rugs and related textiles along with his late wife, Ingeborg.

After graduating from Colby College in Waterville, Maine, in 1963, for most of his working career he was employed in international banking, substantially in Germany and Spain. He has an extensive record of writing in the field of Eurasian ethnographic textiles, including pile-woven rugs, but is best known for the iconic Finch College Museum of Art exhibition catalogue Kazak (1971). Rug study has brought him into extensive contact with cultural anthropology, as well as a myriad of other disciplines, and has afforded him opportunities to speak on the subject of Eurasian weaving in diverse conferences and symposia from San Francisco to Tehran.

An early recipient of the Near Eastern Art Research Center's Joseph V. McMullan Award for scholarship and stewardship in the field of Islamic carpets, he is on the board of directors of the NEARC, which fosters research and publication in the field. His other interests include terrestrial tropical orchids and flora native to the northeastern USA.